Summer Melt

Summer Melt

◆ ◆ ◆

Supporting Low-Income Students Through the Transition to College

BENJAMIN L. CASTLEMAN
and
LINDSAY C. PAGE

Harvard Education Press
Cambridge, Massachusetts

Library of Congress Control Number 2014940440

Paperback ISBN 978-1-61250-741-5
Library Edition ISBN 978-1-61250-742-2

Published by Harvard Education Press,
an imprint of the Harvard Education Publishing Group

Harvard Education Press
8 Story Street
Cambridge, MA 02138

Cover Design: Ciano Design
Cover Image: highhorse/iStock Vectors/Getty Images

The typefaces used in this book are Sabon and Ocean Sans.

CONTENTS

To my mother, Janet Castleman, whose unending support guided me to and through college, and to my wife and children, Celia, Lila, and Simon, whose love and humor fill me with joy each day.

—BLC

To my father, Clem Page, who inspired my college dreams. And to the memory of my mother, Holly Page, who cheered me in reaching them.

—LCP

MELTING DREAMS

For most high school seniors, summer can't come quickly enough. The adventures and excitement that await during the months after high school graduation often culminate the exhilaration of their senior spring: receiving college acceptance letters, planning for prom, walking across the graduation stage. They bid farewell to the days of morning announcements over the P.A. system and daily journeys down hallways lined with combination lockers. Never again will shrill buzzers announce the end of periods. Instead, college-bound graduates imagine the melodious ringing of church-top bells as they stroll across tree-lined campuses. They anticipate their first conversations (or more likely, Facebook chats) with new roommates, shopping trips to purchase dorm supplies, and perhaps one final family vacation before they head off to campus as independent college students.

The post–high school summer has long been treasured as a time for lazy days on the beach and road trips with high school friends before parting ways and continuing on to college. These blissful months have captured the imagination of popular artists, from Olivia Newton-John and John Travolta singing about "summer lovin'" to Katy Perry singing about "those summer nights," while the summer road trip is often-trod territory for Hollywood comedies.

This image of summer bliss resonates with many adults—us included—who fondly recall the post–high school summer as one of the greatest times of their lives. Ben spent two weeks biking around Cape Cod with his best friends—a first adventure away from home and without parents. Days were spent cycling up the coast or swimming in the ocean; nights were spent in youth hostels, meeting other travelers from all over the world. Lindsay remembers summer days working in a retail store to earn money for college, interspersed with day and overnight trips to the Jersey shore with friends—a beginning taste of the independence that life as a newly minted college student would bring.

Many years later, having become friends and colleagues in graduate school, we dove into the summer before college from a more scholarly perspective. Our work led us to the discovery that many hard-working and intelligent high school graduates face a much more trying and turbulent summer of transition from high school to college.

"SUMMER MELT"

Like any good myth, these popular narratives about the summer after high school mask a far more complex reality, when many seemingly college-bound students find that they have to change or even abandon their postsecondary plans. In fact, our research has found that as many as one in five high school graduates who have been accepted to and intend to enroll in college fail to matriculate anywhere in the fall semester as a result of unforeseen challenges they encounter during the summer.[1] We refer to this phenomenon as "summer melt." We distinguish our use of the term from the same phrase that has long been used by higher education admissions officers to refer to the tendency of students who have paid a financial deposit to attend one college to instead matriculate at another, usually presumed to be of peer quality. In some school districts where as many as 40 percent of college-intending students fail to matriculate, it would be more appropriate to refer to this as a "summer flood."[2;3] Although the summer has received little attention as an important time period in students' transition to college, the challenges students encounter during these supposedly carefree months are typical of the barriers that researchers identify as responsible for the persistent inequalities in college entry and success.

Why do students melt? Even after they have been accepted to college, applied for financial aid, and chosen where to enroll, college-intending high school graduates have to navigate a complex array of tasks in order to successfully matriculate. Many of these tasks relate to financing the cost of college. Many students struggle to identify funding sources they can access to cover gaps between their financial aid packages and the full cost of attending their college or university. Students also have to decipher a series of complicated financial forms, from financial aid award letters and supplementary loan applications to tuition bills and payment plan options. This paperwork is daunting for college-educated parents, let alone students who are the first in their family to go to college. Colleges expect students to complete a range of paperwork over the summer, such as orientation and academic placement test registrations, housing applications, advising questionnaires, and health records. In addition, students must handle other logistical tasks, such as arranging and paying for transportation to school for the start of the academic year.

Unfortunately, these tasks come at a time when students typically lack access to professional assistance. They are no longer part of their high school, and high school counselors' contracts usually do not extend into the summer months. Students are frequently unfamiliar with support resources available at their intended college. If a student is the first in the family to go to college, parents may want to help but not know how. Although more affluent students may experience the carefree summer depicted in popular culture, many lower-income students work long hours to support their families financially or take care of younger siblings at the same time that they are trying to manage all the requests from their intended college. Faced with such complex and daunting tasks, lacking access to professional help, and often burdened with other weighty responsibilities, is it actually a surprise that even strongly college-intending high school graduates struggle to achieve their postsecondary dreams?

Of course, summer melt might not be a concern if students were actively deciding to delay college in favor of a short-term alternative, such as a well-paying job. Particularly as the cost of attending college continues to soar, undoubtedly some students are making wise decisions to postpone college while they save additional money or continue to develop their academic and social skills. Yet recent research by Karen Arnold, a professor at Boston College and the person whom we credit for discovering the summer melt phenomenon, suggests that few students are intentionally delaying college to pursue alternative and superior career opportunities.[4] In a survey Arnold conducted of college-intending high school graduates who did not successfully matriculate in the year after high school, nearly half of respondents were unemployed and looking for work during that time. This finding is corroborated by research in another location that followed students who had been eligible for a generous city-based merit scholarship for college but who failed to transition successfully. Of these students interviewed, most indicated they weren't "doing anything with their lives."[5] In both locations, students who were working held jobs primarily in service industries (e.g., fast food and retail sales) with little prospect for advancement.[6]

Recently, policy makers and educators across the country have rallied around summer melt as an important and overlooked barrier to college access for hard-working students from economically disadvantaged backgrounds. School districts and community-based organizations across the map are investing in innovative approaches to reduce summer melt among their high school graduates. Senior officials at the White House and the U.S. Department of Education have increasingly focused on the summer after high school as a period that warrants additional policy focus and intervention.[7] This book dives deeply into the patterns and causes of summer melt and then highlights evidence-based practices that have been employed throughout the country to support students' successful transition from high school to college.

THE FIRST SIGNS OF MELT

Prior to 2006, we, like most of the education community, were largely unaware of the problems and challenges that college-intending, low-income high school graduates encounter during the summer after high school. But a small set of interviews and a pilot program with students from innovative high schools in Providence, Rhode Island, began to shed light on both the magnitude of the summer melt problem and the potential of summer support to help students realize their postsecondary ambitions. At the time, Ben was a school administrator at the Met—the Metropolitan Regional Career and Technical Center—a network of small high schools in Providence. The "college access for all" movement was still gaining momentum. The onus for helping students apply to college rested largely on the family, as schools serving economically disadvantaged populations typically offered only modest college-going supports.

The Met is the flagship district in the Big Picture Learning national network of schools. The Met, and Big Picture schools more broadly, are unique and innovative among urban public schools both for their pedagogy and curriculum and for their approach to college planning and alumni transition support. A core element of the Met philosophy is for each student to have a highly personalized educational experience. In 2006, each Met school had a total enrollment of no more than 150 students across grades 9 through

12. Students must apply to the Met, but they don't need to meet academic benchmarks to gain acceptance. Rather, the district uses a lottery to select which applicants to admit. When they enter the Met, students are assigned to an advisory group with fifteen other students and one academic advisor, and they stay with that same group for the next four years. The Met places equal emphasis both on students' academic preparation and on guiding and supporting their social and emotional development. As a result, students develop extremely close relationships with their peers and school staff, so much so that by senior year, many students say they are closer to their advisors and classmates than they are to their own family. The Met schools' model of engagement has demonstrated impressive results: though three-quarters of the students in the schools are from low-income families, few students drop out, and the graduation rate is consistently over 95 percent.

Another key feature of the Met approach is its focus on preparing all students to go to college. The district integrates the college and financial aid application processes into the senior year curriculum. During senior year, students work on college essays and resumes with their academic advisor, and each student meets several times with a college/transition counselor to review and refine his or her applications.

Though the Met's postsecondary planning philosophy has since evolved to focus more on issues of affordability, in 2006 the district's overriding focus was getting students accepted at and enrolled in the best four-year institutions possible. Though counselors worked individually with each student to complete financial aid applications and review award letters, issues like affordability, debt burden, and college persistence had not yet emerged as hot-button topics within the school. This was pre-recession, when student loan money flowed with the same liquidity as subprime mortgages.

By high school graduation, 99 percent of students had typically been accepted to college. Some of these students decided to work after high school or enlist in the military, but the considerable majority—about 80 percent—planned to enroll in college the following fall. Dennis Littky, the founder of the Met, famously told students at every high school graduation that he was committed to supporting them throughout their entire lives, not just until they walked across the graduation stage. Littky stood behind this commitment and dedicated resources to provide support to Met alumni. College/transition counselors stayed in touch with students in the years following high school, sending care packages to their college dorms and even visiting them on campus when possible. When counselors reached out in the fall after high school graduation, with few exceptions, students who had said they were going to college at graduation told counselors that they were enrolled in college and doing well. The Met was deservedly proud of sending so many low-income students to college; its college entry rate was far higher than the national average for students from a similar background.

Littky wanted to know more than just whether students were in college, however. Were students engaged in and passionate about their learning? After graduating from such a supportive high school environment, was it challenging for them to connect to faculty or support resources? Were they happy? To explore these questions, the Met partnered with Karen Arnold, who had conducted several studies investigating the connection between education and later experiences in adult life. Arnold designed a study to more fully capture the post–high school lives and experiences of Met graduates. Over time, the study gathered rich and detailed information on the experiences of Met alumni through interviews, focus groups, and surveys, but the starting point in the spring of 2006 was an exit survey of all graduating seniors. Via the exit survey, Arnold collected students' perceptions on their Met education, on their readiness for and feelings about life after high school, and on whether they planned to go to college. These survey results confirmed the patterns Met leaders had observed for several years: nearly all students reported being accepted to college (which counselors were able to confirm based on acceptance letters students proudly displayed in school), and 75 to 80 percent reported their intention to enroll.

Arnold did not collect additional data during the summer after high school. For the first time in the school's history though, she did gather external data on students' college enrollment. Whereas Met counselors gathered college attendance information through follow-up phone calls with students, Arnold obtained individual college enrollment information on each of the recent Met graduates from a national college enrollment data source called the National Student Clearinghouse, or NSC.[8] A unique feature of the NSC is that it maintains enrollment and degree attainment information for approximately 95 percent of colleges and universities in the country. Connecting Met students' records to NSC data allowed Arnold to observe whether and where students continued to college, whether they enrolled full-time or part-time, whether they persisted beyond initial college enrollment, and whether they earned a degree and in which field.

This was the first time Met school leaders had the opportunity to see verifiable college enrollment data on their students. What Arnold presented was eye opening, even jaw dropping. Though three-quarters of recent Met graduates reported being in college, the NSC data revealed that just over half of students had actually matriculated. Naturally, Met leaders wanted to understand why there was such a large discrepancy between students' self-reports and the NSC records. College/transition counselors contacted students whom the NSC indicated were not enrolled to see if the data was really accurate. Indeed, many of these students were not actually enrolled in college, despite having told their counselors in earlier conversations that they were. The students said that they were embarrassed about not having made it to college; they were worried that the school would be disappointed in them for not following through on their postsecondary plans.

Met leaders were astonished that some of these students had not matriculated. The students were passionate about continuing their education, had worked hard throughout high school, and in many cases had chosen a quality, affordable college to attend. Just a few short months earlier, they had been enthusiastic about and committed to their postsecondary plan. Arnold and the Met leadership kept coming back to the same perplexing question: What was going on during the summer to lead such promising, dedicated students to abandon their college ambitions?

Until Arnold found the discrepancy between the exit survey results and the NSC enrollment data, the Met had not thought of the summer as an important time period in students' transition to college. Counselors, teachers, and principals assumed that students who paid deposits to enroll in college would matriculate in the fall. Staff of course understood that some students' plans would change, but the assumption was that these changes would result in students opting for a different college—perhaps getting off a waitlist—rather than forgoing college entirely.

This perspective on the summer was largely consistent with the view of most educational practitioners and researchers at the time, which focused on students developing postsecondary plans, considering and applying to specific colleges, and selecting where to attend.[9] This process implicitly culminated on May 1, when students are required to send a financial deposit to hold their spot at their chosen college. High schools' role in this model was to prepare students academically for success in college or the workplace and to see them through to graduation. Families, and to a limited extent high schools, were responsible for helping students explore, apply to, and choose colleges. The work of colleges, then, was to support and retain students once they arrived on campus. And while some colleges do offer or even require summer bridge programs to help students transition from high school to college, they are far from the norm and serve only a small fraction of all entering first-year college students. Within both the secondary and higher education sectors, there was little if any attention to the possibility that college-intending students with specific postsecondary plans at the end of high school would encounter barriers during the summer that would prevent them from matriculating.

Much of our work over the last several years has been to shed light on the extent of the summer melt problem. In the years since Arnold's initial discovery of summer melt at the Met, we and colleagues with whom we have connected on this issue have found melt rates of similar or even greater magnitude in every school district serving economically disadvantaged students where we have gathered data. From practitioners across the country, we have learned that summer melt is occurring among students in large cities like New York, St. Louis, Los Angeles, and Austin; and in rural settings like West Virginia and Montana. Across contexts and throughout the United States, economically disadvantaged and first-generation college-going high school graduates wind up abandoning their college plans because they face challenges they did not anticipate and do not know where to turn for help.

THE PROMISE AND POSSIBILITY OF SUMMER INTERVENTIONS

Despite the barriers that students encounter during this period, several factors point to the promise of focusing on the post–high school summer as a time for concerted effort to increase college going among students from disadvantaged backgrounds and to prepare them to succeed in college.[10] It bears underscoring that the students we are focused on here are college-intending as of high school graduation. First and foremost, these are students who have already accomplished so much: they have persevered through high school, the vast majority have applied and been accepted to college, and in many cases they have successfully navigated the complexities of applying for federal financial aid. Some of these students have benefited from the help of an important mentor but rarely at the level of college-related support that many affluent students receive, either from a parent or from a professional counselor. With a final push to help students overcome obstacles that arise over the summer, we can mitigate melt from a population already poised for college success.

Second, the summer is an ideal time to reach out more proactively to adolescents. Recent work in neuroscience confirms what parents and educators have always known about teenagers: that anything more than ten days into the future might as well be ten light years away.[11] During the waning days of senior year, when students ideally would be focused on preparing for college, there are many more immediate distractions to occupy their attention. In contrast, fast-forward a few months to the middle of summer when students receive their first tuition bill, and college is very much at the forefront of their minds. It is at this point that students are most responsive to outreach from a school counselor. Finally, there is an ample supply of caring and capable people—such as school counselors and near-aged peers currently enrolled in college—who are potentially available and could be hired to provide assistance to students during the summer.

Over the past several years, we have implemented a range of summer college-going interventions in a variety of settings and with a variety of educational partners. Collectively, this work has revealed that a little bit of summer outreach can go a long way. Having counselors invest two to three additional hours per student during the months after high school—or even sending students a handful of personalized text messages reminding them of tasks they need to complete in order to matriculate and offering follow-up support—leads to substantial increases in college access, with the biggest impacts on the most disadvantaged and underserved students.[12] These results are especially encouraging, given how inexpensive it is to provide summer support. Many other college-going interventions cost several hundred if not thousands of dollars per student to achieve meaningful gains in college attendance. In contrast, our summer interventions ranged in cost from just a few dollars per student to send personalized text reminders of summer tasks to $150 to have counselors conduct individualized outreach. Based on this work, we see the summer as an untapped period during which relatively small investments of time and resources by educators and policy makers can achieve sizable improvements in college access among hard-working, low-income students who are highly deserving of and stand to benefit from additional support.

ORGANIZATION OF THE BOOK

In this book, we dive deeply into the problem of summer melt and the steps that educators, counselors, community leaders, policy makers, and researchers can take to prevent this unnecessary loss of talented young people from the college pipeline. We discuss a host of innovative and low-cost strategies that have proven to be effective in mitigating summer melt. Our investigation of this phenomenon highlights many of the challenges facing American higher education more broadly and points to the additional steps policy makers can employ both earlier and later in students' educational trajectories to reduce inequalities in educational opportunities and attainment.

Chapter 1 provides a thorough diagnosis of the summer melt phenomenon. We chart the evolution of our own work on this topic, from when we were first exposed to high rates of summer melt among graduates from one small, innovative high school in Providence, Rhode Island, to our efforts to document the extent of summer melt in school districts across the country. The chapter more comprehensively explores the obstacles that can prevent even strongly college-intending students from realizing their aspirations.

Chapters 2 and 3 illustrate summer melt as experienced by students, school counselors, and community-based staff with whom we have worked and spoken over the years. We rely on their voices and stories to elucidate how students react and respond to the challenges that arise over the summer and how they decide whether to carry through with their postsecondary plans. We weave these narratives together to more fully explore some of the major factors contributing to the summer challenges that college-intending students face. These chapters focus on the financial and informational barriers that students encounter over the summer as well as the behavioral and social-emotional challenges that contribute to summer melt. These include the frustration of having no one to turn to for help or to provide guidance about what needs to get done, as well as the inexorable pull of more immediate commitments and priorities that draw students away from completing the tasks required to successfully matriculate. We also frame students' experiences during the summer after high school in the context of emerging interdisciplinary research about how individuals navigate complex decisions—both in education and in other settings.

In the second half of the book, we provide in-depth profiles of efforts that we and others have launched to mitigate summer melt across a range of educational settings. Chapter 4 profiles a counselor-led intervention in which high school counselors and community-based financial aid advisors reached out to college-intending high school graduates to assess their readiness for college and to help them address any obstacles to matriculation that arose. Chapter 5 profiles how school districts, nonprofit organizations, and state educational agencies have capitalized on the technological innovation of automated and personalized text messaging to support recent high school graduates through the summer college transition. Chapter 6 describes efforts to capitalize on the energy and passion of current college students to support their near-aged peers with summer college-going tasks.

Drawing on these profiles of prior summer melt interventions, chapter 7 provides concrete guidance to school districts and other educational agencies about how they can investigate and address summer melt occurring among their own students. How should agencies assess the magnitude of summer melt among their high school graduates? What data and resources should they enlist to mitigate summer attrition if they do face such a problem? We provide guidance on how education leaders can select a response strategy that is appropriate for the local context and that capitalizes on resources available within their organization. In addition, we provide secondary education leaders with advice on how they can engage local higher education institutions to support students and provide a more seamless transition into college. Finally, in chapter 8, we discuss the implications that the research, programmatic efforts, and student and counselor experiences synthesized in this book have for educational policy and practice more broadly. We also explore the roles and responsibilities that different entities—from students and families to school systems and the federal government—can play to improve educational access and success among our nation's most impoverished students. By investigating the challenges that students encounter during the summer and how educators and policy makers can help students overcome these hurdles, we can not only learn how to better support students through a critical educational transition that has been overlooked to date, but also inform efforts to improve supports for disadvantaged students at many stages in their educational trajectories.

PART I

Understanding
Summer Melt

━━━━ ◆ ◆ ◆ ━━━━

CHAPTER 1

A Trickle or a Torrent?

The Scope of Summer Melt

The study of "summer melt" began with Karen Arnold's ground-breaking work in a small group of alternative schools in Rhode Island.[1] But the patterns that Arnold, a Boston College professor, discovered at the Met Center pointed to a much more widespread phenomenon and helped to identify critical obstacles to students' success.

As described in the introduction, Arnold's comparison of Met students' actual college enrollment to their stated postsecondary intentions only a few months earlier had revealed a striking pattern: nearly one-third of the Met graduates with concrete plans to continue directly to college after high school failed to get there in the fall. Why had students delayed or abandoned entirely the postsecondary plans they had worked throughout senior year to craft? Were students making active and informed choices to put off college in favor of a better alternative, or had they encountered unanticipated barriers and obstacles that derailed their plans? Met leadership had little information to draw upon to answer these questions. At that point, the summer was a black box in students' transition from high school to college; all Arnold and colleagues saw were percentages on a spreadsheet.

The following summer, Arnold set out to understand students' experiences and the barriers they were encountering that led to changes in their college plans in the few short months between high school graduation and the start of the fall semester. Interviews and focus groups with a small group of college-intending high school graduates and counselors from the Met and other Big Picture high schools began to shed light on this puzzle.[2] The thirteen students interviewed had all been accepted to and had paid financial deposits to attend college the following fall. Yet only six enrolled at the school where they had planned to matriculate as of high school graduation. Two students did not enroll at all, one switched from a four-year institution to a community college, and three changed from one four-year institution to another four-year school.

The degree of churn in these students' college plans was noteworthy, but even more striking were the struggles they encountered during the summer months. One of the core challenges that students faced was simply holding on to the dream of going to college. Most of the students interviewed were the first in their family to pursue higher education. They had relied on Met staff not only to guide them through college search and applications, but also to bolster their confidence that they really could succeed in college. What became clear through these conversations was that students viewed their Met advisor and counselors as their north star during senior year, helping them to stay focused on making their college aspirations a reality. During the summer, however, when Met staff members were less present, students' grasp of their postsecondary plans became far more tenuous. Students had yet to fully internalize the dream of going to college. They were torn between the desire to further their education and the lures of home: staying with a girlfriend or boyfriend, receiving a steady paycheck, and continuing to contribute financially and otherwise to their family. Several students reported being pressured from parents and other family members to forgo their college plans. Some parents questioned whether college was really worth the financial investment; others didn't want their child to go far from home and to a new environment—one that was often hard for parents without prior college experience to fully appreciate. Every counselor who participated in focus groups could share a story of a parent who refused or simply didn't have a vehicle to drive their child to college.

The summer after high school was a markedly different experience for the few students whose parents had gone to college. Higher education was never one of several possible post–high school pathways for these students—they always knew that they would go to college directly after high school. One student told Arnold that it never crossed his mind not to go to college. Far from sending mixed or even negative messages to their children, college-educated parents were often the driving force behind their child's college exploration, application, and choice. These parents were willing to sacrifice whatever was necessary—working a second job or taking out personal loans—for their child to have a college education.

Yet nearly all of the students encountered substantial financial struggles during the summer. Though they had all completed the FAFSA during senior year, several students did not receive their award letters until well after high school graduation. In some cases, the award letters were delayed because students were required to provide additional information to the federal government to verify what they had reported on their FAFSA.[3] In other instances, the student's intended college was awaiting additional paperwork from the student or family before sending out an award letter. A few short weeks before their tuition bill was due, these students still lacked a basic understanding of how much financial aid they would be awarded or how much they and their family would be expected to pay.

Even among students who were awarded financial aid—whether federal, state, or institutional dollars—all students faced some level of unmet need between their aid packages and the full cost of their intended institution. Students' decision to change or abandon their college plans sometimes resulted from a lack of confidence that they would ever be able to pay off their loans even if they managed to earn a degree. Other students didn't know how to cover the unmet need that remained after receiving a financial aid package, especially when families were unwilling or unable to assume additional loans. Among parents who were willing to borrow additional money, many lacked sufficient credit to qualify for supplementary loans. Even students who received full college scholarships were not free from financial concerns that arose over the summer. Though they might not have to pay for college, students' departure from home meant that their families could no longer count on the wages they earned or the other supports they contributed. These students often provided essential services at home, such as translating for family members who did not speak English and caring for younger siblings. The offer of a full ride to college notwithstanding, these students were reluctant or unwilling to impose the financial and other burdens on their family that would result if they left.

The final theme that emerged from Arnold's interviews was students' sheer lack of knowledge of the tasks, processes, and requirements—both academic and otherwise—associated with getting to and succeeding in college. Most students did not actively choose to postpone their enrollment. Rather, the opportunity to go to college in the fall slipped from their grasp because they were unaware of or did not know how to complete required tasks. Students often put faith in processes working on their behalf. For example, some students, even if they had not received a financial aid package midway through the summer, assumed that the college was still working on it and would contact them soon. Up until that point, these students were members of a school community that had shepherded them through key educational steps and processes. The complexity and sequencing of the steps required for college matriculation therefore came as a considerable surprise and resulted in substantial confusion.

Faced with so much uncertainty about how to actualize their college plans, some students were easily swayed by their peers' decisions. Despite having no interest in cosmetology, one student decided to go to beauty school because her best friend was going. And while Arnold's investigation preceded much of the attention that the for-profit sector has received for predatory behavior, counselors shared several stories of for-profit institutions aggressively recruiting students during this turbulent and isolated time period.

STEMMING THE TIDE

In the wake of these interviews, Arnold and the Met leadership were collectively struck by the array of complicated challenges students faced and by how little they had previously known about the depths of students' struggles after high school graduation. But they also recognized an opportunity to better support recent Met graduates in realizing their college plans. While the obstacles students encountered during the summer were daunting, few actually seemed insurmountable. The Met could provide ongoing assistance during the summer and continue to guide students through the college process. College counselors could make sure students received and understood their financial aid award letters, help them apply for and evaluate supplementary loan offers, and remind them of other tasks their college would require of them. Counselors could facilitate conversations between students and their families about the student's desire to go to college and help parents better understand how this might benefit both the student and the entire family in the long run. Providing summer assistance wouldn't require hiring additional staff; Met counselors were off contract in the summer months. All that was needed was to extend the contracts of a few counselors for several additional weeks in the summer.

The following summer (2008) the Met tested whether summer counseling support really would lead to meaningful improvements in college access.[4] This is where Ben first had the opportunity to engage with school leaders to mitigate summer melt. As a school administrator, he collaborated with Arnold and Katherine Lynk Wartman, then one of Arnold's doctoral students at Boston College, to randomly assign half of that year's Met graduates to receive outreach from two counselors hired to work over the summer. The other half of students did not receive outreach. Nevertheless, if these students initiated contact with a counselor, they received the same high-quality support. Student response to the proactive summer outreach was striking. Eighty-five percent of the students to whom counselors reached out came in for at least one meeting; over 20 percent of the students who did not receive outreach still got in touch with a counselor because they heard that they were available over the summer. Counselors helped students with a range of tasks, from interpreting their award letters and lobbying for additional financial aid to mediating difficult conversations between students and their parents. Over the course of the summer, the counselors invested only a few hours of time per student but felt that they were able to make a big difference in helping students overcome barriers to their successful matriculation.

The results of the summer outreach were even more astounding. Students to whom the counselors proactively reached out were over 30 percent more likely to enroll in college. In addition, they were also 47 percent more likely to enroll full-time (rather than part-time) and 58 percent more likely to enroll at a four-year (rather than two-year) institution. These latter results were particularly encouraging since students who enroll full-time at four-year colleges and universities are substantially more likely to persist and eventually earn a college degree. The Met's efforts to stem the tide of summer melt might therefore do more than just get students in the door; summer support was conceivably helping to better position students for collegiate success.

In that one summer, Met staff learned that while students' postsecondary plans were vulnerable in the months after high school, they were also highly responsive to the offer of help. Moreover, counselor assistance substantially improved college-going outcomes for the Met graduates. As a result of this work, the Met has provided college transition support to students every summer since.

AS THE MET GOES, SO GOES THE NATION

In hindsight, it is striking how much the experience of this handful of students in one unique school setting in Providence, Rhode Island, resonates with the experiences of students and staff in school districts and college access organizations across the country. In all the settings where we have investigated summer melt, delays in and confusion about the financial aid process pose major hurdles to students' successful matriculation. Depending on when they applied for financial aid, it may be summer before students receive an award letter from their intended college. These award letters are often hard to decipher, leaving recipients in the dark about how much they are receiving in grants versus loans, how much their aid covers relative to the actual cost of attendance, and how much they and their family are therefore expected to pay. If students face a gap between their financial aid package and the cost of attendance, they have to navigate the complex territory of supplementary loan applications. In addition, upon receiving their tuition bills, students are often surprised and confused by unanticipated charges (such as mandatory health insurance and student activities fees) that increase their personal contribution even further. They are frequently unaware of payment options that are available to them, and they are even confused about whether their tuition bill pertains to a semester or full year of college.

As Arnold found in her summer melt interviews, lack of college knowledge poses another substantial obstacle. Students' confusion about required prematriculation tasks during the summer often builds on uncertainty they have faced throughout the college application process. During junior and senior year, economically disadvantaged students are frequently unaware of important steps, such as taking the SAT or ACT college entrance exams.[5] They may be unfamiliar with or lack the college literacy skills to benefit from college search tools, such as the White House scorecard, which are designed to help students identify colleges well-matched to their interests and abilities. They are frequently uninformed about strategies they can employ, like sending their college entrance exam scores and completed financial aid applications to multiple colleges, to increase their chances of being able to attend a quality, affordable postsecondary institution.

Much of this lack of awareness can be attributed to the lack of college counseling in the most under-resourced schools. Nationally, the average school counselor caseload is nearly twice that recommended by the American School Counseling Association.[6] Counselors in public schools spend less than a quarter of their time on college admissions, compared with more than half of available time invested by private school counselors.[7] Paradoxically, students from low-income backgrounds tend to have the fewest connections to family members or other adults knowledgeable about how to apply to college, while students from high-income backgrounds typically have the most access to sophisticated college counselors. Some affluent families pay private consultants thousands of dollars to guide their child through the college application process. For example, a four-day college-application "boot camp" run by a former admissions officer of an Ivy League institution costs $14,000.

As in Providence, most college-intending students from lower-income backgrounds are even more isolated from quality information or professional assistance during the summer after high school. They have graduated from high school but are not yet part of their college community. High school counselors typically work on nine- or ten-month contracts and are not available to provide support even if students seek it out. In addition, many colleges and universities now disseminate important matriculation information via online portals. Yet students are often unfamiliar with these portals or overlook the login information that their intended college sent them in earlier correspondence.[8] Limited Internet access during the summer months may create a more basic problem: low-income students may simply not be able to view the paperwork that their college expects them to complete. As a result, many of the forms that students are required to submit prior to matriculation remain untouched as the summer marches on. As one college transition counselor summarized, the issue is "students not knowing what to do when challenges come up. Many students feel they are in a state of limbo before they start at their new school and after they have graduated from high school. They aren't sure who to ask for help and instead choose not to ask at all."

When we describe these informational barriers to researchers and policy makers, common questions typically follow: "Don't students know there are forms they have to complete? Why aren't they reaching out to their college to find out what they should be doing? If they can't get these tasks done over the summer, how could they possibly be successful in college?" While there is some validity to these questions, the underlying reasoning overlooks the fact that adolescents of all socioeconomic backgrounds often struggle to manage the college process: immediate pleasures nearly always trump long-term planning or attending to onerous responsibilities; task management and organization are rarely strong suits; and many teenagers benefit from a responsible adult in their lives to provide direction (and frequently prodding) about what has to get done in the college process. Students from college-educated families typically have parents who stay on top of them during the summer to make sure they complete all college-related requirements or who handle college-transition tasks on their child's behalf. In contrast, first-generation and lower-income students often face the substantial challenge of navigating the complex college process on their own.

Consider two eighteen-year-olds with identical grades, test scores, and extracurricular experiences, but who differ in that the parents and grandparents of the first student all went to college, while the second student is the first in his family to do so. Neither student typically has access to professional guidance over the summer. This is unlikely to be a cause for concern for the first student, as his parents will probably shepherd him through the financial aid documents and other paperwork he must complete. In fact, intense involvement of highly educated parents in their children's college experiences has become so ubiquitous that the term "helicopter parent" is now a standard part of college administrators' lexicon. The second student is often in a more challenging situation. Without professional guidance regarding required tasks, and lacking family members who can provide direction or support, he is more likely to be adrift and unaware of what is expected.

Perhaps what makes the summer after high school unique is that it is a distinctly "nudge-free" time in students' educational trajectories.[9] During high school, students receive detailed guidance from their teachers about what assignments to complete and when each is due. In many communities, there are increasing efforts, such as the national College Goal Sunday campaign, to prompt students to complete key aspects of their college applications. Even in college, students' professors and teaching assistants provide considerable direction, in the form of syllabi and weekly sections, about the work students should be doing. During the summer, however, students frequently do not receive any such direction or personalized outreach.[10] In addition, the nature of these tasks is different from the academic work to which students are more accustomed. In the absence of such nudges and supports, students may miss important deadlines, such as registering for orientation, or have too little time at the end of summer to complete everything that is required. In sum, many students who overcome the numerous hurdles to get into college find in the eleventh hour that they can't actually enroll—not because they were lazy or unmotivated, but because the educational system has not provided support during this crucial period of transition.

A TRICKLE OR A TORRENT?

Despite the overwhelming success of the Met summer pilot experiment, it remained unclear whether other schools should adopt the Met approach and work with students in the summer after high school graduation. Several open questions remained: How similar were college-intending graduates from the Met to college-intending students elsewhere? The Met actively supports students through the college application process. Students in less-supportive environments have to be much more self-motivated to apply to college. Would students from other schools therefore be more facile at navigating the challenges of the post–high school summer and less susceptible to summer melt? In addition, the Met is a unique educational setting in which students have intensely close relationships with staff and are accustomed to getting regular calls and e-mails from their advisors and other staff during the academic year. Would students in more mainstream educational settings be similarly responsive to summer outreach? Ultimately, it remained to be determined whether summer melt was a broad problem or largely confined to these unique schools.

It was around this time that we, Ben and Lindsay, became friends in graduate school, discovered our shared interest in improving college outcomes for students from disadvantaged backgrounds, and began to wrestle with these questions together. With the Met work as a foundation, we embarked on an investigation of whether summer melt was a problem that educational systems beyond the Met experienced. With an enthusiasm possessed only by doctoral students hungry for data, we set our sights first on understanding the magnitude of summer melt across the country. Just as soon as we started, however, we promptly hit a wall. Quantifying summer melt was no easy task. Doing so would require linking information on students' college plans with data on whether and where they enrolled. However, few districts administered high school exit surveys at the time, and those that did were not eager to share their data with a couple of graduate students. In addition, none of the national sources of data and information collected by the U.S. Department of Education explicitly asked graduating students whether and where they planned to attend college.

The limitations of the national data sources notwithstanding, our first attempt to measure summer melt at a national scale relied on data available through the Educational Longitudinal Study of 2002.[11] This study provides information on a nationally representative sample of approximately 16,000 students who were interviewed as tenth graders, as twelfth graders, and once again two years after their expected high school graduation. The twelfth-grade interviews, which were most important for our purposes, were conducted over a several-month period during the spring of senior year in high school. Though the survey information did not include a direct measure of students' college intentions as of graduation, the available data did allow us to narrow down the sample to those students who had applied and been accepted to college. Among these students, we further focused on those who had applied for financial aid at the college(s) to which they had been accepted, as an additional indicator of their intention to pursue postsecondary education. Through the follow-up interviews conducted two years after high school, we were then able to learn whether students whom we had identified as college-intending actually matriculated in the fall semester following high school.

What did we find from this initial inquiry into the extent of summer melt? A trickle of change, or perhaps even a steady thaw, in students' college plans over the summer—but certainly not the degree of churn and tumult that had emerged from the Met studies. Virtually all of the students who were best positioned for college—possessing strong academic credentials and from higher socioeconomic backgrounds—matriculated in the fall following high school. On the other hand, melt was more prevalent among those with lower academic ability and socioeconomic status; among college-intending students who were economically disadvantaged and who exhibited average academic performance, 85 percent enrolled immediately after high school.

However, we didn't necessarily expect to observe extremely high rates of melt among a nationally representative sample of college-intending high-school graduates. These students were wealthier, on average, than the Met student population, and were more likely to have college-educated parents who could provide assistance during the summer months. Furthermore, because of how we defined college-intending students, most of our sample intended to enroll at four-year colleges and universities and had all successfully completed the Free Application for Federal Student Aid (FAFSA). If college-going plans were more tenuous for students who planned to attend community college or failed to acquire financial aid, our Educational Longitudinal Study analysis was largely missing those pieces of the puzzle, and therefore resulted in what could arguably be considered a lower bound on the extent of summer melt. What we really wanted was to investigate the magnitude of summer melt among a population similar to the Met students in background but from a more mainstream educational environment.

Our first opportunity to do so came in our own backyard through a partnership with a Boston-based college access organization then known as ACCESS and now called uAspire. uAspire runs several programs to help students prepare for college, apply for financial aid, and select an affordable postsecondary option. Of particular interest was uAspire's Last Dollar Scholarship program, which provided supplementary grants to students to help defray the difference between their financial aid package and the cost of attending their intended school. Students applied for the Last Dollar Scholarship just before high school graduation. To be eligible for the award, students had to have worked with a uAspire advisor during the academic year, have been accepted to college and applied for financial aid, and most importantly for our purposes, have decided where they planned to enroll.

The Last Dollar Scholarship applicant pool presented a golden opportunity to investigate summer melt. The applicants came from every public high school in Boston, and so represented a broad range of urban educational experiences. Students were predominantly from low-income families and typically had little access to college planning support at home. In addition, they were as college-intending as high school graduates could be—not only had they applied, been accepted, and decided where to enroll, they had also completed the FAFSA and taken the initiative to apply for a supplementary scholarship. Eighty-five percent of Last Dollar Scholarship applicants planned to attend four-year colleges and universities and the remaining 15 percent, local community colleges. We knew where they planned to enroll as of high school graduation, and thanks to data obtained by uAspire from the National Student Clearinghouse, whether and where they actually matriculated.

Simply on the basis of their prior preparation for and determination to attend college, one might have expected melt rates as low or lower than in the national sample. Instead, however, the picture that emerged from our analyses closely resembled the patterns found among Met graduates. Among the Last Dollar Scholarship applicants who intended to enroll in a four-year institution, more than one in five did not matriculate anywhere in the fall after high school. Among students who planned to attend community colleges, two in five failed to do so.

Similar patterns of summer melt have since been detected in public school districts across the country. In Fulton County, Georgia, as in Boston, one in five college-intending students failed to enroll in the fall after high school. In Dallas and Philadelphia, upwards of 30 percent of college-bound students did not matriculate. In several other cities, including Lawrence, Massachusetts, and Fort Worth, Texas, the melt rate approached or exceeded 40 percent.[12]

Not surprisingly, melt disproportionately afflicts the lowest-income students, who may very well stand to benefit the most from a college education. In Boston, for instance, only 6 percent of middle-income, college-intending students failed to realize their college plans, compared with 24 percent of students from the lowest-income families.[13] The disparity in melt by socioeconomic status was even more pronounced in Fulton County, Georgia. While only 7 percent of non–low income students melted, 37 percent of those from economically disadvantaged backgrounds failed to matriculate in the fall. In Fort Worth, these rates were 26 percent and 58 percent for nondisadvantaged and disadvantaged students, respectively. Across these three sites, the melt rate for lower-income college-intending students was two to five times as great as for their more affluent peers.

Disparities in summer melt by socioeconomic status reflect broader economic inequalities in college access and success. Students from lower-income families are less likely to enroll in college, less likely to attend a college that is well-matched to their academic abilities, and less likely to earn a degree than students from higher-income families.[14] That these gaps have only widened over time is of particular concern. Although other factors, such as differences in academic preparation and college affordability, certainly exert a large influence on the persistence of these inequalities, the challenges that low-income students encounter during the summer also contribute to the stubborn gaps in college access and success with which the United States continues to wrestle. Alleviating this eleventh-hour loss from the college-going pipeline is therefore an important component of a broader strategy to equalize educational opportunity for the nation's students.

At conferences and convenings, in phone calls and e-mails from district personnel and college access leaders, we learn of melt rates in other locations that are just as high and that disproportionately affect low-income students. Summer melt is as prevalent in rural contexts like West Virginia and Kentucky as it is in cities like Hartford and Los Angeles. Even if only 10 percent of all college-intending, low-income students melted each year, this would equate to enough students to fill the largest football stadium in the country, at the University of Michigan with capacity for 109,000 spectators, more than twice over. Imagine every seat occupied by a bright, hard-working student on the cusp of a college education, only to have their postsecondary plans forestalled by unanticipated and unfamiliar challenges.

———◆—◆—◆———

CHAPTER 2

Three Students, Three Summers
Navigating the Transition to College

When asked about the factors that contribute to summer melt, counselors rarely offer explanations such as students' lack of academic ability or lack of determination to realize their college aspirations. Instead, their responses suggest melt is primarily a function of circumstances that are outside of the students' control—the socioeconomic and educational status of their families and communities. Students from college-educated families are more likely to receive constant support and direction through the summer months. When these students encounter challenges during the transition to college, their parents are more likely to intervene and help them stay on track. College-educated parents often take charge of figuring out how to pay for college, help their children wade through college paperwork, and facilitate communication with their child's intended college.

Students with strong parental support can thus focus more of their attention on the activities typically associated with the transition to college: connecting with roommates, purchasing dorm supplies, and exploring the course catalog. In short, these students are able to socialize to college in a way that students from lower-income families frequently cannot. As the profiles in this chapter illustrate, a lack of access to this level of consistent and informed parental guidance often plays a major role in whether college-intending, low-income students are able to realize their college plans.

This chapter looks into the lives of Adam, Tarik, and Alicia, three recent high school graduates who planned to enroll in college for the fall semester.[1] Adam grew up in a large, middle-class family in the Midwest. As a young child, Tarik emigrated from Ethiopia to the United States and completed all of his elementary and secondary schooling in a New England town. Alicia grew up in a lower-income family and completed her high school years in a large midwestern city. Juxtaposing the summer experiences of these three students provides a window into how personal and family circumstances contribute to whether students are able to successfully navigate the summer transition to college.

ADAM

"Adam, you need to find a job. You're not going to waste the entire summer playing video games!"

"I know, Mom, you already told me. I'll start looking this week."

"You'll start looking today. Until you have a job, all you're doing is driving your brothers and sisters to their activities. No going out and no time with your friends."

"Enough already. I got it."

Such was the typical exchange in Adam's household at the start of summer. Since high school graduation, his parents had been insistent about him getting a summer job. He hadn't held a job throughout high school, and his parents felt it was time he develop some responsibility before heading off to college. Adam didn't disagree—he just wasn't overly motivated to look for work.

Adam was far from lazy; he had excelled in high school, played on several sports teams, and pursued various math and science enrichment activities. His hard work had paid off, earning him a spot at a prestigious private university in the Northeast. Now the start of college was a few months away, and Adam was enjoying his freedom and unstructured time. He came from a large and close-knit family and didn't mind driving his siblings to swim practice and other activities. "In the mornings I was a chauffeur," Adam said. "In the afternoons I mainly read and messed around."

Adam's parents owned a small consulting business. They worked hard, were successful, and managed their schedules so that one of them was always at home. In the weeks after high school graduation, this also meant that one of them was always maintaining the pressure on Adam to find a summer job. Adam would often leave the house under the pretense of looking for work but instead spend time with his girlfriend. When his parents finally demanded that he do something productive, Adam lined up a few middle-school students to tutor in math. This was enough to satisfy his parents for at least a few weeks.

Though he wasn't overly focused on finding full-time employment, Adam was on top of college-related tasks. Whenever he received paperwork from the financial aid office, he would bring it to his dad, who would "handle all the numbers stuff from there." Adam's financial aid application was somewhat complex. His father had completed the basic aid applications, but given the structure of the family business, Adam's college requested additional information. Even after Adam's parents submitted all requested forms, however, the college still expected them to pay more than they felt was affordable. Adam has six siblings, and though his parents' consulting business was successful, his parents did not feel that the government's estimate of what his family could contribute aligned with the cost of raising seven children. His parents were very proactive about reaching out to the financial aid office at the college, explaining their circumstances and appealing to the college to provide more grant aid. Their persistence paid off: the college provided additional financial assistance. Going to college was never really in question for Adam or his family; even without the additional institutional grant aid, they would have assumed the loans necessary to allow Adam to pursue his college plans. But the supplementary funding made it possible for Adam to enroll without imposing financial stress on his family's budget. Even at the time, he was grateful to his parents for these efforts. "As a high school senior, there's no way I would have been comfortable going back to the college and saying, 'Can you give me more money?'"

With his finances worked out and enough tutoring clients to keep his parents at bay, Adam was able to focus for several weeks on getting ready for college. He spent time going through all the courses the college had to offer. "This was the first thing I realized I had complete control over," he said. He had countless interactions via Facebook with other incoming freshmen. Several years after the fact, Adam still remembers how excited he and his soon-to-be suite mates were when the college posted dorm assignments, and he could see which building he'd be living in when he arrived on campus. He and one of his new roommates had multiple conversations about what to bring for their dorm room. By the end of July, the only mild source of concern for Adam was the prospect of spending over twenty hours in a family van from the Midwest to a family vacation spot on the Atlantic coast. He would spend two weeks with his extended family on the beach and then have a couple weeks to pack up before flying off to school.

The possibility that his college plans might fall through never occurred to Adam. This is because he had ample time to focus on the college transition process, and had the support and involvement of his parents to handle the financial aspects. The possibility of college plans slipping away might also never strike the minds of students with very different family circumstances. Not because they have everything in place, but instead because they lack an awareness of the critical pieces of information that they are missing. Once students gain this understanding, however, it can sometimes be too late to catch up.

TARIK

Tarik's parents came to the United States from Ethiopia when he was a young child. They settled in a small New England town and took various blue-collar jobs to support their family. They were committed to working hard and to supporting Tarik in his academic career. They had never been to college but sought for their son the upward mobility that more often came with a college education. During his senior year, Tarik worked diligently on both his schoolwork and on his college applications. His high school provided a great deal of support and guidance throughout the application process, and Tarik felt confident that the schools to which he applied presented good opportunities for him. Tarik and his family celebrated the successful submission of his college applications, and Tarik was able to enjoy the final months of his high school career, hopeful that a great college option would be available to him the next fall.

The celebration within Tarik's family continued when he was accepted to a public college in their state. Both he and his parents were delighted, reveling in the bright future Tarik had ahead of him. Not having returned to Ethiopia for many years, Tarik and his parents traveled back home for several weeks in the summer to visit with family and friends and to celebrate Tarik heading off to college in the fall.

Tarik and his family returned to the United States later that summer, tired from their journey but fulfilled by their time with friends and relatives. Soon after arriving home, they sat down together to sift through the weeks of mail that had accumulated. Tarik had expected some correspondence from his college, but the volume surprised him. As he opened the many envelopes, a knot grew in his stomach. With each piece of mail, Tarik realized that he had missed several deadlines related to fall matriculation: placement tests, orientation, housing paperwork. Though Tarik found these forms a bit daunting, he was fairly clear about what was required of him.

Tarik's tuition bill, on the other hand, was much harder to decipher. Given his family income, Tarik would have qualified for a substantial amount of financial aid, including a Pell Grant. Yet he had never even completed the FAFSA—not because he shirked this responsibility, but because he didn't realize that it existed. As Tarik recounted, "I thought that I was prepared, but there was so much that I didn't know. I didn't even know about the financial aid system. My parents and I didn't know what financial aid was. It would have helped to have support from someone even after getting accepted." While his high school had provided substantial support with the college application process, it did not provide assistance with financial aid. Tarik was unaware that the application for financial aid should have been next on his list after submitting his college applications.

Tarik was a motivated student and so reached out for help from the college academic advisor that another piece of mail indicated was assigned to him for the upcoming school year. After talking with his advisor, however, Tarik realized just how far behind he was and how much more college would cost him than if he waited a semester and applied for financial aid. Following the guidance of his college advisor, Tarik opted to delay his enrollment. While he remained determined to get to campus, his college plans would have to wait until he had the financing to afford his postsecondary education.

For Tarik, it was a lack of awareness about financial aid that hindered his college plans. Even for students fully aware of the financial aid application process, however, small bumps along the way are equally likely to derail their college plans.

ALICIA

High school graduation was still several months away, but for Alicia college couldn't come soon enough. She had accomplished what no one else in her family had done: she had applied and gotten into college. It hadn't been easy—Alicia's mother passed away during her freshman year, and she hadn't had a stable place to live throughout high school, instead moving between her brother's and father's apartments. Alicia's relationship with her father was complex. Sometimes he was helpful and supportive, but he could also be unreliable and unavailable. But Alicia was bright, hard-working, and tenacious. She was about to graduate from an urban public high school in the Midwest with both a strong academic record and several college acceptance letters in hand. Now, Alicia was just waiting to see which college would offer her the best financial aid package. She was on the verge of realizing her college dreams.

Senior year advanced. A long midwestern winter slowly relaxed its grip, and Alicia was looking forward to the senior activities leading up to graduation. April arrived, and Alicia still hadn't received her financial aid award. Not for any lack of effort on her part, however. In fact, Alicia had been working to complete her financial aid application since shortly after the New Year. She made sure her father filed his taxes as soon as he received his W-2s at the end of January. Soon after his tax returns were complete, she logged on to the U.S. Department of Education (USDOE) FAFSA website to complete her financial aid application.

The FAFSA filing process should, in theory, have been more straightforward and less time-consuming for Alicia than for students in prior cohorts. In response to research documenting how complexities in the FAFSA application process can deter academically qualified, low-income students from going to college, the USDOE has in recent years undertaken several initiatives to simplify the process. One of the more innovative strategies has been to allow most aid applicants to prepopulate the online FAFSA application with information they or their parents provided to the IRS in their electronic tax returns.

Alicia tried to make use of the Internal Revenue Service (IRS) tax retrieval tool during her FAFSA submission. She closely followed the prompts to transfer her father's tax information into her FAFSA application, providing his name, social security number, and address. She double- and triple-checked her entries to make sure that everything was accurate and clicked to submit.

Much to her surprise and confusion, however, Alicia received an error message saying that the IRS tax retrieval tool could not locate her father's information. She rechecked the fields that she had entered to confirm everything was accurate and clicked to submit again. But still the retrieval tool did not work. The only option the website provided to Alicia was to hand enter information from her father's tax returns. Alicia didn't know if her father had kept a copy of his records and wasn't sure when she would next see him to ask for the paperwork. She was skeptical whether she would be able to get a copy of the tax returns directly from her father, so she decided to request that the hard copy be sent via postal mail to her father's apartment.

Two weeks went by, and the tax documents still had not arrived. As busy as Alicia was during senior year, finishing up course assignments and getting ready for senior prom and class trips, she never lost focus on completing her aid application. Alicia had a connection to a college access organization in her community and asked her college coach for advice. He hadn't encountered this problem before, however, and wasn't sure why the tax transcript hadn't been delivered. Every couple of weeks, she submitted another request for the tax documents, but to no avail. High school graduation was fast approaching, but Alicia still didn't know how much aid each college would offer her. She wondered whether the colleges would still be able to offer her as much financial assistance, since she had missed their priority deadlines for completing her FAFSA. Still, she was determined to enroll in college and had a clear sense of which institution she wanted to attend. But she felt like her postsecondary plans were on hold until she had financial aid packages to review and compare. Alicia asked her father for a copy of his tax return, but he had not kept one after filing his taxes. In a last-ditch effort, Alicia looked up the location of the closest IRS office and persuaded her father to go in person to request his tax returns.

After months of unsuccessful attempts to get the tax documents, this strategy proved successful; finally, Alicia was able to obtain a copy of the tax returns. And in doing so, she and her father realized why Alicia's efforts to request the documents online hadn't worked. To retrieve the records, the IRS officer asked her father to verify the information on his returns. His name and social security number were correct, but he had accidentally switched two numbers of his address when he had submitted his taxes. This trivial error had prevented Alicia's online requests from being successfully processed, since the (correct) address she entered online didn't match what the IRS had on file.

Alicia completed her FAFSA as soon as she was able, but didn't receive her award letters until July. She had only a few weeks before the start of the semester and faced a daunting set of decisions and complex processes to navigate: whether she could afford to live on campus, if any housing was still available; whether she and her father would need to apply for additional loans; how she would scrape together the remaining balance on her tuition bill, which incidentally arrived within a week or two of her award letters.

Alicia's story fortunately had a happy ending. She was one of the lucky few students in the country who had access to high-quality college advising during the summer, through the college access organization with which she had connected during senior year. Coaches from the organization were able to help Alicia manage these decisions and processes and successfully matriculate. But in many communities across the country, a student in Alicia's position would not have access to summer college counseling and would have faced substantially longer odds of successfully enrolling.

Though they had profoundly different family and lifestyle circumstances, Adam, Tarik, and Alicia were not so different from each other. They were all bright, had all worked hard in high school, and were all looking forward to the promise and excitement of college life. Each encountered challenges, particularly related to the financial aid process, between college acceptance and college matriculation. Where their paths diverged largely had to do with the adult support (or lack thereof) in their lives. Adam's role was limited to passing on the financial aid paperwork to his parents; they handled the rest. Tarik and his parents, by contrast, were not even aware of the financial aid process, while Alicia worked tirelessly to complete her applications but ran into challenges nonetheless. Had she not worked intensively with a college coach in the final weeks of the summer, it is unlikely that her college plans would have come to reality.

The summer after high school entails an intricate series of financial and procedural tasks that students must complete in order to matriculate. As the portraits of these three students demonstrate, with strong family supports in place, these tasks are typically manageable—and sometimes barely noticeable. In the absence of guidance, however, and particularly if students don't have school- or community-based resources to which they can turn, even seemingly minor problems can derail a student's college plans. We turn now to exploring in greater detail, again through individual student stories, the many ways in which students' postsecondary plans can fall off track in the summer months prior to matriculation.

◆ ◆ ◆

CHAPTER 3

"Summer Melt Begins in February"
Punctures in the College Pipeline

Consider for a moment how Alicia's college transition might have been different and less harried if her father had more experience with the college-going process or if she had had more access to college advising during the academic year. If he had known he would need his tax information to complete the FAFSA, Alicia's father might have kept a copy of his completed returns. In that case, even if the tax retrieval tool had not worked, Alicia would have been able to manually input the necessary information. A parent more experienced with the college process might have been more proactive about getting the tax returns, perhaps by calling the FAFSA hotline for help or seeking out advice from a tax or financial aid professional in the community.

Either of these fairly straightforward actions would have set in motion a cascade of important events. Alicia would have completed her FAFSA and received her award letters months earlier, likely qualifying her for financial aid packages more generous than the ones she ultimately received. With concrete information about her financial aid in hand, Alicia also would have been able to apply for housing earlier, increasing the probability that she would receive on-campus housing. With financial aid and her college decisions completed, she would have been able to focus more fully on other tasks, like attending orientation, completing academic placement tests, and connecting with her roommates, all of which contribute to a successful start to freshman year.

As Alicia's story and those of the students introduced in this chapter illustrate, the sequence of steps students need to take in the months leading up to matriculation can be conceived of as a kind of pipeline. Small punctures in the pipeline, either individual or cumulative, have the potential to derail students' plans. Many summer tasks are sequential, so an early and unanticipated delay like the problem Alicia faced with the FAFSA can produce a domino effect of additional delays and new challenges that compound the problem and even become insurmountable. As one college advisor put it, "summer melt begins in February." Alicia was perhaps unusually attuned to the tasks required for successful transition to college. Yet, as this counselor shared, it's more typical that students think the college chores are over once they have completed their applications. Many students don't realize that applying for financial aid is a separate process. For others, applying to college is in itself so challenging that they are exhausted and struggle to maintain focus on additional tasks, like applying for aid. Students' motivation often returns as high school graduation approaches and acceptance letters arrive, but by then they may have missed the critical window of opportunity for setting important processes, like financial aid, in motion. "From January to college enrollment," this counselor explained, "it's a roller coaster for kids," with many "tapped out" by the struggle to navigate this new terrain without sufficient guidance or support.

MINOR OBSTACLES CAN LEAD TO MAJOR DERAILMENTS

Unfortunately, Alicia's experience typifies the challenges that many college-intending, low-income graduates face during the summer months. Her college plans were on the verge of falling apart not because she lacked motivation or determination. Nor was college simply unaffordable for Alicia. Her aid package (inclusive of federal loans) was sufficient to cover the cost of her tuition bill. Rather, like many would-be first-generation college students, Alicia encountered challenges that could have led her to delay or entirely abandon her college plans. Some students, like Alicia, are very much on top of the college choice and matriculation process but don't know where to turn for help when challenges arise. Other students, like Tarik, are equally determined to pursue postsecondary education yet are less familiar with the important stages in the process of successfully enrolling in college. Students are frequently unaware of when required tasks are due or may even be unsure about whether they have successfully completed a particular step. For example, a common reason why some students fail to fully complete their FAFSA application is that they do not perform the electronic signature step properly.

Further, students' lack of experience with or confidence in navigating complex bureaucracies means that they are more hesitant to proactively reach out to their intended college or to community-based resources for help. They may be reluctant to give the impression that they don't know what is expected of them for fear that college staff will question whether they are really ready for higher education. If they do reach out to an admissions or financial aid staff member for assistance, they may be stymied by an initial negative response and not know how to further probe with additional questions. For instance, a student might call her college's residential life office to ask if she can submit her housing form without the application fee. Such conversations often end when the student is abruptly told, "No, we cannot process your housing application without the fee," because the student doesn't know what questions to ask to explore whether any accommodations are possible (e.g., waiving the fee or applying the fee to the term bill so it can be covered by financial aid). Given that many admissions and financial aid offices are understaffed relative to the volume of correspondence they receive, students are also often intimidated when staff members are brusque or rushed over the phone, and may not feel comfortable posing additional questions or asking for clarification.

Moreover, many students from low-income backgrounds lack access to adults who have the knowledge and experience necessary to help them identify, organize, and keep track of various processes and tasks and who can help navigate bureaucracies to access professional help when challenges arise. As a result, information students should receive during senior year, like their financial award letters, often doesn't arrive until well into the summer, putting students in the position of having to scramble when faced with the financial reality of paying for college. Compounding the problem, these students may have only intermittent Internet access over the summer, or may have to share a computer with multiple family members, and so may not stay on top of college correspondence. Delayed information may prevent students from completing other processes, like applying for housing. Lower-profile summer tasks, like orientation, placement tests, and signing up for student health insurance (or waiving it if they already have coverage), may go unnoticed because students missed an e-mail reminder or didn't log on to their student web portal through which colleges increasingly disseminate important information. Either individually or collectively, these minor obstacles can derail the postsecondary plans of accomplished students with high capacity for collegiate success.

It is worth pointing out that many of the tasks that students need to complete over the summer draw on a set of skills—the ability to digest and complete financial forms or the self-advocacy necessary to navigate bureaucracies—that few students develop in high school. For many low-income students, the transition to college requires that they take on primary responsibility for complex processes like income verification and loan applications that are challenging even for college-educated adults. As one counselor explained, "There is so much immediate, sudden independence that students get, and they don't know how to manage that. For the students who aren't assertive, who don't know what they need, or don't know how to go after what they want, they can get lost in the shuffle, especially when they don't even know where to start."

"THESE KIDS HAVE NO SAFETY NET"

While it is important for all students to mature into these skills of self-sufficiency, it bears emphasizing that high school graduates from more affluent backgrounds often are not any better at managing and completing this complex array of summer tasks—they just have more help. To transition to and succeed in college, students from low-income backgrounds often must quickly assume adult roles and responsibilities. In contrast, their wealthier peers are more likely to enjoy an extended period of adolescence during which their parents continue to manage many aspects of their college experience.

Lower-income students experience at least two key disadvantages in the college-going process. First, because their circumstances often are less straightforward, the steps that are required of them can be more complex. As a charter school director of college initiatives said, "Many of our students have different-from-typical household situations. Yet, the process is set up for students from 'typical' family situations."

Shanice's experiences exemplify this point. Shanice attended an urban charter high school in the Northeast. Early in her high school career, she became estranged from her parents. Though her parents moved to a neighboring state, Shanice maintained her residency and continued to attend the same high school through the support of friends and other relatives. Shanice was a strong student and earned acceptance to the state flagship university. Yet, because she was still legally a dependent of her parents, and they lived in a different state, the university charged her the out-of-state rate for tuition and room and board—nearly twice that for in-state residents. Shanice didn't know how she could possibly afford to attend.

Unlike many public high schools in the United States, Shanice's charter high school offered a more robust college-advising staff. "You wouldn't believe the hurdles to getting her counted as an in-state student," the school's counseling director recounted. "She had never even been out of the state!" With the support of her counselor, Shanice had to work well into the summer to correct this misclassification and convince the university to count her as an in-state student.

The second disadvantage that students from lower-income families typically face, as noted above, is that their families and social networks lack familiarity with the college-going process. In contrast to more affluent students, whose parents frequently direct and monitor all that has to get done in order to matriculate, low-income students often must navigate the college process on their own. As one college counselor stated, "Up until students [of all backgrounds] go into the 'adult' world, there is a lot of enabling that goes on. Students hand things in late; a lot is tolerated. Lack of responsibility and tolerance for that is something that happens across the board with teenagers. Other students may have well-educated parents who are able to intervene, but these kids have no safety net."

College-educated parents understand the steps their children need to complete in order to matriculate. Their knowledge likely comes from a combination of their own personal college experience, their social networks, and their willingness to actively read and seek out information from the colleges themselves. They develop a high degree of college literacy, which allows them to shepherd their children through the process. In contrast, first-generation students and their families often lack this college literacy and are therefore more likely to stumble on the pathway to college.

LEAKS IN THE PIPELINE: INCOME VERIFICATION

As Alicia's story demonstrates, summer obstacles can originate much earlier, with the financial aid application. However, FAFSA-related problems can also arise after students have completed their aid applications if they are flagged for income verification. These students are required to submit additional documentation to verify the income and asset information that they reported on their FAFSA. This information includes the number of people in the household, the number of these people who are attending college, income and child support amounts, and tax documentation, such as W-2 and 1099 forms. It is commonly reported that approximately one-third of FAFSA filers are identified for income verification each year.[1] However, several community-based college access organizations have reported much higher verification rates for the students with whom they work. They cite two primary factors that seem to predict whether a student will be asked to verify their income. The first is an unconventional source of income. Students whose parents work multiple jobs or who receive income from extended family members appear more likely to be flagged, as do students whose families receive government transfers or income support, such as Temporary Aid for Needy Families or food stamps.

The second trigger for income verification is an unconventional family structure or living arrangement. For example, students might still legally be a dependent of both parents but live with a grandparent, aunt, or uncle. In other cases, one or both of a student's parents may be away from home for extended periods and only contribute income irregularly, if at all.

Tiona had lived in foster care since she was thirteen. Throughout high school, she worked several jobs a year, usually two at a time, just to support herself. When it came time to apply for financial aid, Tiona was able to apply as an independent filer, meaning she did not have to submit parental income information. To verify her status as an independent when she completed her FAFSA, she was required to submit her own W-2 as well as formal documentation of her foster status. She submitted this paperwork but was nonetheless flagged for verification. At first, she thought it meant that she'd made a mistake on the FAFSA. She then discovered that she was required to file her taxes before she could finalize her

FAFSA, but didn't know how or where to go for help. Her aunt finally agreed to take Tiona to the location where she filed her taxes but only if Tiona agreed to give her a portion of her refund.

Although it is the federal government that selects students for verification, students complete the verification process directly with their prospective colleges. Tiona therefore had to complete separate verification documents for each of the colleges that had accepted her. Several of the schools sent her additional forms with which to verify her status as an independent. Though Tiona's first-choice institution required that she complete multiple verification forms, the financial aid office's policy was to send her one form at a time. Only after she completed and returned each form would they send her the next one. Tiona's initial response to the stress and complexity of the verification process was to simply ignore the forms that kept arriving. With support from a college access organization she was able to connect with over the summer, however, she eventually cleared the verification process. Tiona successfully matriculated to a state university.

As the director of college completion at one college access organization pointed out, the FAFSA verification process often disadvantages the very students that need-based financial aid programs are designed to support. Students who live with both parents and whose family income is reported largely or entirely through W-2s are less likely to be flagged for FAFSA verification. This means that they receive their award letters sooner and have more time to compare aid packages across institutions and to pursue additional funding, if necessary. Knowing how much aid they qualify for, students may be able to apply for housing earlier in the year, and are more likely to secure a residence hall spot before all spaces are filled. Because students with unconventional sources of income, family structures, or living arrangements are more likely to be flagged for verification, however, they may also be more likely to miss priority deadlines for institutional financial aid. These same students, in turn, may not receive their financial aid packages until the summer, which gives them very little time to secure any additional funding needed and to complete other tasks in time for fall enrollment.

FINANCIAL AID CONFUSION

While income verification poses a challenge for some students, others are able to navigate this step relatively quickly, and still others are not flagged for verification. Many college applicants receive their aid packages without a hitch; if they filed early enough in the year, they may even receive their award letters well before high school graduation.

Even with award letters in hand during the school year, however, students frequently encounter financial aid challenges during the summer. Some of these struggles stem from misunderstandings about scholarships, grants, and loans or from confusion about the award letters themselves. As one current college student recounted, "When I opened the [award] letter, I was like, 'What is this?' All I saw were names of companies and numbers. I was like, 'Is this how much I need to pay, or what they're giving me?' . . . I just didn't know what to do . . . I just saw dollar signs." One reason for this confusion is that the considerable majority of students do not receive any financial aid counseling prior to high school graduation. Many public high school students have limited access to college counseling, in part because school counselors have myriad responsibilities for large student caseloads. Given the number of students for whom each counselor is responsible, the average high school student might expect to get about fifteen minutes of individualized college-going support during senior year, at best. Moreover, most of the school counselors with whom we have worked report that they themselves lack a thorough understanding of the financial aid process and, without further training and professional development, do not feel confident assisting students and families with steps such as evaluating financial aid packages. As a result, many students, even if they receive award letters during the school year, don't review them with an informed adult in detail, or at all. This means that students often go into the summer without a clear understanding of how much aid they will be receiving and what gap they may face between their aid package and the cost of attending their chosen institution.

To understand why students often are confused by their award letters, put yourself in the shoes of a first-generation college-bound student. You have applied and been accepted to college and have recently received your financial aid award letter in the mail. The summary of your award looks something like table 3.1.

The first two rows of the table are fairly straightforward. The top line is clearly labeled a federal grant, and the second line is clearly labeled a federal loan. What about the third and fourth lines? Is a student who is the first in his family to go to college and who has received limited financial aid counseling likely to know that "Subsidized Stafford" and "Unsubsidized Stafford" refer to loans rather than grants? The fifth line may also be cause for confusion. Would the student necessarily know that the $2,600 in federal work-study has to be earned once he is in school and cannot be applied to the fall tuition bill? Finally, the total award amount, $39,600, is a lot of money. The student might reasonably conclude that this covers the full cost of attending the institution, but the letter does not actually make this clear, since it does not include a separate figure for the total cost of attendance.

Table 3.1: Sample summary of financial aid award

	Fall 2012	Spring 2013	Total
Federal Pell Grant	$750	$750	$1,500
Federal Perkins Loan	$1,000	$1,000	$2,000
Federal Subsidized Stafford	$2,750	$2,750	$5,500
Federal Unsubsidized Stafford	$1,000	$1,000	$2,000
Federal Work-Study Program	$1,300	$1,300	$2,600
President's Award	$13,000	$13,000	$26,000
Total awards	$19,800	$19,800	$39,600

Note: We adapted this sample financial aid summary to look similar to numerous financial aid awards we have reviewed over the years.

To the federal government's credit, the USDOE has taken several steps to improve the clarity of financial aid award letters. In July 2012, the USDOE unveiled the Financial Aid Shopping Sheet, a standardized award letter format designed to simplify information about different components of financial aid and the total cost of attendance and to make it easier for students to compare aid packages across institutions. USDOE encourages but does not require institutions to use the Shopping Sheet. As of summer 2013, only about a third of colleges and universities were formatting their award letters to look like the Shopping Sheet rather than what is presented in table 3.1.

A lack of clarity about the award letter can lull students into a false sense of security. Students who think their aid package covers the full cost of attendance are often caught off guard when they receive a tuition bill in July or early August that has a substantial balance. The same can happen to students who misinterpret work-study as a credit that will be applied to their tuition bill at the start of the semester. Students who fail to distinguish loans from grants sometimes decide to delay or abandon their college plans when they discover they will have to pay back thousands more dollars in loans than they initially realized. And even students who think that the entire cost of attendance is covered by scholarships are sometimes in for rude surprises.

During his senior year, Ryan applied and was admitted to a branch campus of his state university system. As the valedictorian of his high school, an urban public school in the Northeast, Ryan earned a prestigious scholarship to cover the full cost of his tuition as well as provide a small stipend for daily expenses and books. As soon as he received this scholarship, he provided the information to his intended college. With this funding, Ryan believed his college costs would be fully covered.

What Ryan's scholarship did not provide, however, was support for housing. At first, Ryan didn't anticipate this to be a problem. The branch campus he planned to attend was in his hometown. He would simply commute to college each day, living with and being financially supported by his grandmother. Early in the summer, however, Ryan's grandmother told him that, now that he was on his way to college, she planned to move to another part of the state to be closer to other friends and family. Her decision to move put Ryan's college plans in serious jeopardy. He wouldn't have a place to live once his grandmother relocated, and he didn't have the funds for room and board elsewhere. Although his mother lived in the same town, she was pregnant with another child and made clear to Ryan that he was on his own financially once he turned eighteen. Now that he was legally an adult, she no longer received child support for him. Therefore, he could neither live with her nor could he count on her to obtain loans to support his living expenses. Ryan's opportunity to take advantage of the valedictory scholarship that he had earned felt like it was slipping away.

During this time, Ryan was lucky to have continued his relationship with the local college access organization. Ryan shared his concerns with his college advisor, who was able to work with Ryan and his grandmother and help her understand what college could mean for Ryan's future, and what chaos her departure would create for his hard-earned plans. As the director of the college access organization noted, "This was the critical moment . . . our ability to interact with the family and to coach Ryan on how to speak to his grandmother. This is what he could not have gotten elsewhere. Because of the conversation between Ryan, his advisor, and his grandmother, Ryan's grandmother decided to postpone her move so that Ryan would be able to remain living with her and continue with his postsecondary plans.

Students and parents also typically assume that whatever financial aid they have been awarded will be applied in advance of their tuition bills. Their logic is straightforward and understandable: if they receive $16,000 in total aid and the cost of attendance is $20,000, they should only have to come up with an additional $4,000 to pay the full bill. Students and their families are routinely surprised, therefore, to learn that this simple logic doesn't always hold. For instance, in order to release federal loan funds to the institution, students need to complete online loan counseling and fill out a Master Promissory Note (MPN). Many students put off doing this until the end of summer, which means that the loan dollars are often not credited to the fall tuition bill that students receive in late July or early August. Depending on when students complete the MPN, they may be expected to pay the balance out of pocket and be refunded once the loans are applied to their account.

Even students who receive enough aid to cover the full cost of attendance are often caught off guard by what they are expected to pay up front. For example, a student might receive an aid package for $30,000, while the cost of tuition, fees, room, and board is only $28,000. The student can then use the $2,000 balance to pay for textbooks, a computer, or travel to/from home—other expenses that are often factored into the total cost of attendance. However, many institutions don't issue students the balance of their aid packages net of tuition, fees, room, and board until late September or early October. Even if they know this check is coming, many low-income families don't have sufficient liquidity to lay out a couple thousand dollars up front. Thus, students in this situation begin their semester behind—without the books and computer access needed to excel in their coursework.

Ryan encountered a similar situation as he was preparing to start the fall semester. In addition to the full tuition scholarship that he was awarded, Ryan received a smaller scholarship from a local family foundation. This scholarship was not sufficient to cover living expenses in the event that his grandmother moved, but it would allow Ryan to make purchases that would help him be a more successful student. For example, the foundation agreed, in principle, to support Ryan's purchase of a smartphone with a hot spot so that he would have reliable Internet access. This was critical, because Ryan was a commuter student and did not have Internet at home. In fact, advisors raised lack of Internet access as a challenge faced by many students who do not live in a college residence. Yet, the purchase of the phone and hot spot would not be covered or even reimbursed directly from the foundation, as a foundation trustee deemed a payment directly to a vendor of smartphones to be an inappropriate distribution of scholarship funds.

Ryan was fortunate to again be able to call on the college access organization in his community. When he discussed the issue with his college advisor, the organization agreed to purchase the phone on Ryan's behalf. The foundation was more comfortable with distributing the scholarship funds to an organization that was obviously college related. The director of the college access organization explained this unapologetically: "We have been laundering funds associated with that scholarship for years. We bought Ryan's phone and the foundation was able to reimburse us directly because we sound more 'college-y' compared to [the local] smoke shop, where we actually bought the phone." As Ryan's experience illustrates, it's often more challenging than one would think to access scholarship dollars even after they have been awarded.

Even when students manage to pin down exactly how much aid they are receiving and how much they will owe on their tuition bills, paying the gap is rarely as easy as a parent writing a check for the balance. Students often have to cobble together money from various sources: additional loans they or their parents take out, money they borrow informally from extended family members, or earnings they generate from multiple summer jobs.

TUITION BILL SURPRISES

Students often face similar confusion when interpreting their tuition bills. They are often surprised by the balance on the bill, either because they assumed their total aid was equal to the cost of attendance or because they did not anticipate the additional charges that would appear. For example, origination fees are applied to several types of federal loans, making the actual loan amount that students receive smaller than expected. In some cases, unanticipated charges can be quite sizable. For instance, health insurance fees are typically $1,000 or more; they are often not referenced on award letters but are sometimes automatically added to the tuition bill. Students may not realize that they qualify to waive this fee if they can remain on their current health coverage.

In still other cases, unanticipated fees on the tuition bill can be relatively small but still difficult to manage and often unnecessary. For example, certain college campuses that are entirely nonresidential by default include parking fees of $40 to $60 per semester on students' tuition bills. Even fees at this level can threaten the stability of students' plans. As one college counselor reflected, "Students need to take care of so many tedious things and processes that will otherwise cost them. Oftentimes, however, they don't know to pay attention to these details. It's really necessary to coach students to go line-by-line on the bill. They need to make sure that each charge actually applies." Because students frequently have little experience deciphering complicated financial bills, they sometimes just misinterpret the information.

Students can also face difficulties in accessing their tuition bill in the first place. Julia received an award letter from her top-choice institution fairly early in the summer. During high school, an advisor had recommended that she check her aid package against the cost of attendance to see how much she would owe. Julia's award letter provided an estimate of the balance she would face on her tuition bill but not an exact cost of attendance. She knew there could be additional fees (like health insurance) and wanted to know what the actual bill would be so that she could make sure to save enough over the coming months. When Julia called the financial aid office, she was told her bill wouldn't be available until she registered for classes at orientation. While this order of events is not standard for all institutions, it is becoming more common as colleges differentiate charges based on whether courses entail additional costs for materials or activities, such as labs.

Unfortunately, Julia couldn't figure out how to get to orientation. Her family couldn't drive her the three hours to the campus, the bus didn't leave early enough to get her there on time, and she couldn't afford a hotel if she took the bus the day before. She would have to register for classes when she arrived on campus at the beginning of September and could neither view the bill nor waive the health insurance charge (in favor of her current coverage) until then, despite the fact that the bill was supposed to be paid in early August. Faced with uncertainty about how much she would owe, Julia had her parents apply for a Parent Plus loan from the federal government. Their application was denied due to insufficient credit, which automatically increased the total amount Julia could borrow directly by $4,000. Between these additional loans and a payment plan Julia set up to spread payments over a several-month time period, she was able to pay her fall bill and enroll for the semester.

As another student's story illustrates, even simple misinterpretations, if uncorrected, have the potential to derail students' plans. Juanita was excited to have been admitted to a selective private institution. She had applied for financial aid early in the year and had received a generous aid package. Though she and her family would owe a small balance, she felt confident they could cover the difference. When Juanita received her tuition bill, however, her jaw dropped. The total charges were listed as $20,000 for the fall semester alone. Juanita started to panic. There was no way her family could come close to covering that gap, even if she took out additional loans. Juanita became despondent; she figured her only option would be to attend the local community college and maybe transfer down the road. But she couldn't motivate herself to complete the straightforward community college application, even though it was much simpler than the application to her first-choice institution.

A couple weeks after she received her tuition bill, Juanita received a call from a financial aid advisor with whom she had worked during the year. The advisor was calling to check on her plans to enroll at the private institution. Juanita told him that she had given up on that option because there was no way her family could afford a $20,000 bill. This sounded like an unrealistically large amount to the advisor who, knowing Juanita's academic record and income level, thought her gap should be small or non-existent. Through this conversation, he helped Juanita to understand that she had misread the bill. She was focusing on the total charges, rather than the amount due net of financial aid. Once her loans were applied, Juanita owed just a few hundred dollars for the fall semester.

"IT'S THE LITTLE THINGS THAT ARE THE BIG THINGS"

Even if students are able to scrape together enough money to pay their tuition bills, they usually do not have much, if anything, to spare. Small but unanticipated fees, some of which arise early in the summer, can prevent students from completing important and often mandatory summer tasks. Paul, a student from the southwestern United States, encountered this challenge while he was preparing to enroll at the public four-year university in his city. The university, like many in the country, requires that students attend an orientation prior to the start of the fall semester. At the orientation, the university provides students with an overview of the academic options and support services available; students also have the opportunity to meet with an advisor and register for fall semester courses. Paul was excited to attend the orientation. He figured he would meet other students who would be starting the term with him and would get a better sense of what the college was like. But Paul didn't have the money to pay the orientation fee required to register. He was already asking his family to help out with college and didn't want to ask for more money that he was pretty sure they couldn't afford.

The first few orientation dates passed by, and Paul started to question whether he'd be able to start in the fall. He happened to talk to a school counselor from his high school, who told him that he could charge the orientation fee to his term bill and use his financial aid to pay for it. Paul did so and was able to attend orientation, but without this helpful tip from his counselor, he might never have learned that this payment option existed.

Kevin's college aspirations were similarly threatened by a minor cost obstacle. He worked hard through graduation and was admitted to his first-choice school, the state flagship. This campus is very popular and frequently does not have sufficient housing for all incoming freshmen. When it came time to apply for housing, Kevin completed the application but was surprised to see that he had to pay a $25 processing fee. He didn't have $25 and so submitted the application without it, planning to pay the fee once he had the money. What he did not understand was that housing would run out quickly, and his application would not be processed without the fee. Every day that Kevin delayed submitting the fee, he reduced his chances of securing on-campus housing.

Sure enough, by the time Kevin checked on the status of his application, the on-campus housing had entirely filled up. His only option was to live off campus, but he didn't know the college neighborhood or how to search for housing. Kevin would have given up and enrolled at the local community college were it not for last-minute assistance from a community-based college advisor who helped him to find an apartment near campus. As one college coach explained, for these students, "it's the little things that are the big things." Seemingly trivial costs, in particular, can become a major threat to students' college plans.

In addition to the many financial obstacles that students encounter during the summer, several procedural hurdles can make matriculation difficult. As noted earlier, many colleges now disseminate important information related to financial aid and required summer tasks through online portals. Colleges typically provide the login information for these portals with students' acceptance letters and sometimes resend the login credentials via e-mail closer to high school graduation. Yet college-intending students typically are not in the habit of checking these portals over the summer. And even if they are aware (and many are not) that the college is distributing time-sensitive information to the portal, they often cannot locate their login credentials. They may not remember that the information was provided on the acceptance letters they received in early spring, and e-mails from their college are frequently buried in in-boxes that they check sporadically, if at all. As one college counselor explained, "I keep on my students to check their e-mail accounts, to initiate their student accounts, and to stay on top of the many notices that pop up. I recognize that if students don't keep up with a given step, they will be barred from completing the step that follows, and I try to drill this into them."

Another bureaucratic hurdle that students encounter is finding someone at the college to talk to when they encounter a challenge. Take, for example, a student who has a question about a health insurance charge on his tuition bill. Up until that point, any financial information the student received from the college likely came from the financial aid office, so he might start by trying to contact an aid officer. At most public colleges and universities, financial aid offices have only a handful of staff members to field questions from thousands of students. And these offices are usually in skeleton-crew mode in the summer as staff members take vacations. The student might have to leave several voice messages and persist in calling back before connecting with someone, only to be told to contact billing since the question relates to the tuition bill rather than to financial aid. Billing offices are also often understaffed, so the student might again need to make several calls before reaching someone. In some cases, he might be redirected yet again to the office that handles health insurance plans and waiver requests for the college. Frustrated with such convoluted systems, one student remarked, "Students do need to be more accountable for themselves, but it would be good if we could better understand what we need to do and who we can contact for help."

Navigating these financial and bureaucratic hurdles would be challenging for any adolescent, regardless of his socioeconomic background. But several contextual factors make these summer tasks particularly daunting for low-income students. More specifically, social and family contexts often exacerbate the summer barriers that college-intending students face, and contribute to more pronounced rates of summer melt among those from economically disadvantaged backgrounds.

MANAGING A BALANCING ACT

One of the primary challenges low-income students face is completing required summer tasks while balancing a multitude of additional responsibilities. This juggling act is challenging enough when students have received financial aid by the start of summer; it often becomes overwhelming when students don't receive award letters until July and have only a few weeks to complete all that is required while also managing other responsibilities such as working and taking care of siblings.

Andrew began the summer well versed in this balancing act. Growing up, he lived with his mother and young brother, though their living circumstances were always highly unstable. They moved between cities and Andrew attended three different high schools. For two years, Andrew and his brother lived in a foster home because their mother was unable to care for them. During Andrew's junior year of high school, the family ended up in a homeless shelter for several weeks before relocating to a transitional apartment. Andrew's mother came in and out of their lives as she struggled with various health and substance abuse problems. While Andrew saw other students immersed in youthful frivolity like sports practices and late-night adventures, Andrew and his brother were shuffling from one temporary home to the next: their older brothers' apartments, the homeless shelter, and a youth service agency.

Though Andrew experienced neglect and abuse, he was a constant and reliable source of protection and support for his younger brother. He worked nearly full-time to support his family but still maintained his goal to graduate not only from high school but also from college. He finished high school with a 3.0 GPA and performed well enough on the ACT to earn admission to a selective college in the Midwest. But life started to unravel during the summer after high school. Each day brought a new scramble to figure out where he and his brother would be sleeping that night. He was logging countless hours to help his mother qualify for a Section 8 housing voucher, which would provide his mother and brother with a more stable and sustainable living situation. Andrew was also working long hours to make ends meet and save for college, and he struggled to devote time to enrollment tasks. He had no Internet at home and had a hard time staying on top of what his college expected him to complete. He was at risk of losing an outside scholarship he had received unless he could complete his FAFSA verification, since the scholarship organization required a copy of his award letter as part of its eligibility criteria.

Andrew knew that he should be dealing with these tasks but found that he kept putting them off while he dealt with more immediate priorities. This pattern continued well into midsummer, by which time Andrew started to doubt whether he would be able to enroll in the fall. Were it not for the sustained efforts of a college access organization in his community, it is unlikely that Andrew would have matriculated. As part of their standard practice, advisors at the organization work with each student to identify, walk through, and complete each outstanding task. They also gave Andrew access to a computer and phone so he could communicate with his college directly, and helped him purchase dorm supplies. By the end of the summer, Andrew had completed all of his prematriculation tasks and had also helped his mother successfully qualify for the Section 8 voucher. He could start his freshman year in college with some peace of mind that his brother now had a consistent home to return to each night.

Why did a student who persevered through so much adversity in middle and high school to fulfill his college dreams procrastinate on completing these requirements? On the one hand, delay is a common response for many of us when faced with complex and onerous tasks. But according to research by two behavioral economists, Sendhil Mullainathan and Eldar Shafir, individuals from economically disadvantaged backgrounds are often so cognitively depleted by making ends meet each day that the additional energy and attention required to deal with complex processes may exceed their capacity.[2] Mullainathan and Shafir find that in a variety of settings, both domestically and internationally, people who live in impoverished situations usually have to allocate a substantial portion of their cognitive attention to immediate and short-term demands. In Andrew's case, these demands included finding a place to sleep at night and scraping together enough money to feed himself and his brother each day. As a result of devoting substantial energy and attention to these pressing needs, students like Andrew have less cognitive capacity to deal with tasks such as finalizing their financial aid, seeking out additional funding, and navigating complicated procedures.

"IT'S HARD TO BLAME THE PARENTS; THEY ARE JUST TRYING TO SURVIVE"

Students from low-income backgrounds also frequently receive markedly different messages from their family and friends about going off to college than do students from more affluent backgrounds. The messaging in middle- and upper-class families is often clear and unequivocal: Go to college. Go to the best college you can get into. Go to the college that feels right. By contrast, students from lower socioeconomic backgrounds receive ambiguous messages and sometimes even negative pressures related to their college plans. Some families have strong financial reasons to encourage their child to stay at home. The family might depend on the student's wages to pay bills or might need the student to take care of younger siblings, as was the case with Andrew. The family may also see having the child stay home as a cost savings, if it means not having to take out loans or use family savings to pay for tuition. There may also be cultural reasons for why parents prefer to have their child stay home rather than live on a college campus. As one college counselor explained, "Many families see education as a luxury—something that is 'nice to have' but not a necessity. It's hard to blame the parents. They are just trying to survive."

Even when parents with limited resources push their children to continue to college, students sometimes feel guilty that they are "leaving their family behind" when it comes time to depart for campus, as one college counselor explained. "Many students face a difficult decision [either] to go off and place a temporary financial burden on themselves and on their family or to stay at home and work one or two jobs and support their parents and siblings. The summer months leave plenty of time for students to fall into the guilt they feel and to make the decision to stay and support their family."

Some counselors have expressed concern to us that in certain cases, families may even attempt to exploit the financial aid for which students qualify. Recall Ryan, the student who received multiple scholarships. One of the awards came to Ryan in the form of a tuition refund once he was enrolled for the fall semester. When he got the check, for $3,500, Ryan's college advisor expressed immediate concern that his family might seek to access these funds for their own needs. To help Ryan protect these finances for his college education, the advisor took him to the bank to open his own account.

Carlos had a hard time convincing his family to support his plans to go to a college six hours from home. His father had been sent to prison when he was a young boy, so Carlos's grandmother raised him. Although his father was released while he was in high school, Carlos continued to live with his grandmother. After all the turbulence of his childhood, Carlos saw college as an opportunity to try living somewhere else. He wanted to attend a four-year college and wanted to live outside the city in which he had grown up. He was accepted at four different schools, but most of his family—his father, brothers, aunts, and cousins—were opposed to his leaving home. They were nervous about his grandmother living on her own, and didn't think Carlos would be safe so far from his family. No one in the family had left the city before, and they couldn't understand why Carlos wanted to. Six hours seemed like a long way, and the family didn't know how Carlos would get to campus. Carlos's father was reluctant to help him complete the

FAFSA. He told Carlos that he could help him get a scholarship for the local community college and that he didn't need to apply for financial aid.

Many students would struggle to persevere with their plans in the face of such concerted family pressures, but Carlos was determined to go to college. Over the course of several long conversations, he persuaded his grandmother to support him. She became his family advocate and brought the rest of the family on board with his plans.

FROM COLD FEET TO SUMMER MELT

For some students, the pressures to not enroll are internal rather than external from family or friends. Some students begin to doubt in the months after high school whether they belong at college, or increasingly worry that they will have a hard time relating to their new classmates. Other students, when faced with the concrete prospect of leaving home in a few short weeks, are concerned that they will have to give up certain aspects of their identity to fit in on campus. It can be particularly challenging for students to go to college if they perceive that they are the only one from their neighborhood who is leaving home. One counselor hypothesized that "melt happens because students don't have the confidence or they don't feel like they are prepared to take the steps that they need to take."

One counselor, for example, shared the story of Serena, a student who had taken all of the right steps to get to college during high school. Serena had applied, was accepted, did all of her FAFSA paperwork, and was awarded great financial aid. Over the summer, however, "she went AWOL." Serena's college counselors were not able to reach her, but noticed that on Facebook she was posting about how college wasn't necessary to be successful in life. When they finally contacted her, they discovered that Serena feared failure and was afraid of letting down the people who had supported her up until that point. "She just froze—a paralysis out of fear," her counselor recounted. Serena wasn't the only student to have this reaction. Her counselor could recount similar stories for several students, and wondered openly about the extent to which issues of summer melt are wrapped up in issues of identity and a fear of belonging.

Even for students who manage to complete all that is required of them during the summer, the simple challenge of getting to campus can stand in the way of their successful matriculation. Jada's parents couldn't take time off from work to drive her to school, so she looked up public transportation options online. She saw that she could take a train to one city and then a bus from that city to the college. What she failed to realize until the day before she was scheduled to leave was that in the connecting city the bus station was several miles from the train station. She didn't have money for a taxi between them and didn't know how she'd lug all her stuff across town. Luz, meanwhile, had a full ride to college but no ride to get there—her mother didn't own a car, couldn't afford a rental car, and couldn't take time off work to drive her even if she could borrow a car. Both students might have had to give up on their college plans were it not for a college access organization that was able to get Jada taxi fare and Luz a ride to school. For other students who plan to live at home and attend college, transportation is a daily issue. One student shared that she failed to enroll in the fall because of the logistical barriers of daily travel. She didn't have a car or a license and so had no way to get to campus each day.

Most of the students profiled here and in chapter 2 were fortunate to have access to college planning supports during the summer. Yet, given the rates of summer melt documented in chapter 1, it is clear that not all college-aspiring students currently have such critical support. In part II, we devote several chapters to describing a variety of strategies to help more students like those we profile in this chapter to realize their college aspirations.

PART II

Mitigating
Summer Melt

CHAPTER 4

———◆ ◆ ◆———

Capitalizing on Counselors
Summer Outreach Within and Outside Schools

A key element of the eventual success for the students profiled in the prior two chapters was the presence of a caring, knowledgeable adult who was able to help them with college-related tasks and challenges that they faced in the summer after high school graduation. For students like Adam (chapter 2), parents play this role. But for many other students, parents are unable to provide the guidance and support their children need to realize their college aspirations, given their own lack of literacy with college-related processes and tasks. For others still, parents are simply unable or unwilling to lend assistance because of their own challenging circumstances and/or competing needs. Students like these need the support and expertise of other knowledgeable adults to navigate the process.

In chapters 4, 5, and 6, we discuss a variety of intervention strategies focused on supporting students through this summer transition. Common across all of these interventions is the aim to provide students with timely outreach, simplified and personalized information about the tasks that they need to accomplish, and individualized assistance with these tasks to keep them on track for college.

One promising strategy is to capitalize on the existing professional staff in schools and other college-focused organizations. School counselors, to the extent that their school-year workloads allow, are at the forefront of supporting students with the college-going process. Continuing their work through the summer months is a natural extension of their existing professional responsibilities, and the summer may be a period where they are uniquely able to focus their attention on their recent graduates' college transition, rather than on the multiple competing demands they face during the school year. Therefore, extending counselors' direct work with students, as in the Met intervention, may be a viable strategy to fill the void of support that students face and to reduce summer melt, broadly speaking.

uAspire, the college access organization introduced in chapter 1, adopted this approach in responding to the summer melt experienced by the students it serves via its Boston site. The large majority of students with whom uAspire works attend the Boston Public Schools; a substantial portion of uAspire students have not only gotten into college and received financial aid packages by the end of senior year, they have also applied for additional scholarships to help defray remaining unmet financial need. After examining scholarship applicants from the graduating classes of 2007, 2008, and 2009, uAspire learned that over 20 percent failed to realize their plans to matriculate to college directly after high school. This finding caught uAspire by surprise. Fortunately, this discovery did not lead to inertia. uAspire's leadership is action and innovation oriented and, together with us as research partners, quickly began to intervene and improve rates of college matriculation among its future cohorts of college-intending students.

uAspire was well poised to implement a new and successful summer outreach effort. It is an extremely well-run, mission-driven, and student-centered organization. Of particular relevance to supporting students during the summer was the fact that uAspire advisors were twelve-month employees. Compared to the academic school year, during which advisors regularly traveled to and worked within area high schools to help students make financially viable postsecondary plans, summer responsibilities were typically less intense and involved less interaction with students. Advisors spent the months of June, July, and August planning and preparing for the upcoming school year, working on special projects or new initiatives, and taking the time to rejuvenate through some well-deserved vacation. While some of the advisors had contact with students over the summer months, this was not uniform across advisors and typically did not result from systematic outreach efforts. More often, summer contact emerged from close connections that some students had made with their uAspire advisor during the school year. Direct student support was not viewed as a key component of advisors' work over the summer, and therefore they were not proactive or systematic in reaching out and offering support. As with counselors from the Met, uAspire advisors were under the presumption that students were following through on the postsecondary plans that they had made by graduation.

Advisors' availability over the summer was an important factor because it meant that a high-quality staff was already in place to support students. In addition, advisors had strong relationships with the students they worked with during the academic year, recently updated contact information for these students, expertise on financial aid, and a central location for meeting with students. In short, uAspire was a setting in which a larger-scale summer counseling initiative was readily feasible.

Still, given advisors' other summer responsibilities and uAspire's existing strategic initiatives, it was not a foregone conclusion that advisors would have sufficient time and energy to devote significant time to providing outreach and one-on-one support to students over the summer. Therefore, we worked closely with uAspire leadership, particularly CEO Bob Giannino-Racine and president

Erin Cox, to design a summer outreach program that would be feasible for uAspire to implement in its Boston office.

PLANNING FOR SUMMER COLLEGE CONNECT

The key concept for the summer outreach was straightforward— uAspire advisors would provide outreach and support to college-intending students who had been served by uAspire during the academic year. With that goal set, active planning for the beta version of uAspire's Summer College Connect (SCC) was under way. uAspire would implement and staff the effort; our role was to collaborate on designing the counselor outreach strategy and to conduct the research to understand its impact on students' college-going outcomes. Still, several key questions were yet to be answered: How would advisors reach out to students? What would they say? How often would they reach out and how many students could each advisor reasonably serve? What if advisors had students who were dealing with issues that extended beyond uAspire's organizational focus on college financing and affordability? How would advisors react to participating in an effort that had both a programmatic and a research focus?

While we had studied summer melt for some time, the uAspire advisors certainly knew far more about the day-to-day issues and challenges that students confronted in advancing their college plans. Summer College Connect would require a substantial shift in the structure, pace, and expectations of advisors' summers. The success of the initiative depended on their insights and especially on their buy-in. The planning process therefore drew deeply on advisors' expertise and experience.

Three core themes emerged from conversations with and insights from the uAspire advisors. First, uAspire recognized that student and family decisions about postsecondary education, and about college financing and debt in particular, were deeply personal. The uAspire advisors did not want to be in the position of offering specific recommendations lest they be misconstrued as decisions that the advisors were making on a student's or family's behalf. Rather, the advisors saw their role as facilitating students' transition to college with full information and understanding of the decisions they were making and the steps they still needed to take to make their college plans a reality.

A second theme that emerged was the need to interact in a such way that students would feel neither patronized nor enabled by advisors' outreach and support. For example, while advisors were wholly committed to guiding students through the tasks required for successful matriculation, they were emphatic that they would provide coaching and scaffolding rather than complete the tasks themselves while the student looked on. This approach ensured that the summer meetings were an opportunity for students to gain hands-on experience resolving barriers to their college aspirations and to practice self-advocacy. The summer work was to build students' college literacy as well as their capacity to identify, organize, and tackle such tasks in the future.

The third theme came in the form of Erin Cox's regular reminder that, from her perspective, "not all summer melt is bad" if it means that students are carefully evaluating financial decisions and avoiding overly risky or ill-advised options. Thus, if advisors were able to help students fully understand the implications of accruing high levels of college debt and build a more financially viable college plan, even if this meant delaying enrollment, this was a win in uAspire's eyes.

This philosophical foundation laid the groundwork for a host of materials and guidelines to structure and support advisors' work with students over the summer. At the start of the summer, advisors were to conduct an assessment meeting with each student to gauge the financial feasibility of their college plans and to identify required tasks and potential barriers to successful matriculation. Advisors would then work with each student to identify the next steps to address these challenges. These initial interactions were to happen soon after Summer College Connect outreach began in late June, and advisors would encourage students to meet in person for the assessment conversation. We anticipated that students would need help with tasks such as reviewing their financial award letters, logging on to their college web portals, and reading through paperwork they had received from their intended college. It simply didn't seem practical to provide this type of support over the phone. Further, uAspire's high school advising program was built around in-person, one-on-one meetings.

Given its organizational focus on college affordability, uAspire expected that questions and concerns related to financial aid would frequently arise over the summer. A natural question, for example, was whether students with unmet financial need should contact their intended college to lobby for additional grant aid. Holly Morrow, uAspire's director of network programs, had developed useful criteria for classifying the monetary gap between students' financial aid packages and their total cost of attendance. Morrow codified these criteria in uAspire's "Appeals Cheat Sheet." As for additional grant aid, advisors would generally support reaching out to the institution if the student faced low levels of unmet need (e.g., $2,000). For students with moderate levels of unmet need (closer to $10,000), advisors would help identify supplementary loan options. Finally, related to Cox's stance on the potentially positive aspects of summer melt, if a student faced a level of unmet need greater than $12,000, advisors would initiate a frank conversation about the longer-term financial viability of such college plans.

While uAspire advisors had substantial expertise to help students navigate financial aid issues, they had less experience guiding them through some of the other procedures, such as housing paperwork and attending campus orientation, described in chapters 2 and 3. It quickly became obvious that providing advisors with general information on how to help students was insufficient, given that these tasks varied considerably from one institution to the next. Instead, advisors needed more detailed, institution-specific guidance on the procedural steps required of students prior to matriculation. This recognition prompted the creation of "college transition cheat sheets"—single-page, college-specific summaries of all of the tasks incoming students needed to complete in the summer prior to matriculation. In appendix A, we provide an example of a college transition cheat sheet for Bunker Hill Community College.

At first blush, assembling these cheat sheets seemed daunting, given the number of colleges and universities in the Boston area. But the vast majority of students served by uAspire planned to attend one of about fifteen schools, most of which were within twenty miles of Boston. These included public four-year institutions, such as the University of Massachusetts campuses in Amherst, Boston, Dartmouth, and Lowell; the local two-year institutions of Bunker Hill Community College and MassBay Community College; and a variety of private institutions, including Boston College, Boston University, Newbury College, and Regis College. Perhaps unique to the Boston higher education market, which is rich with postsecondary options, fully half of the uAspire students intended to enroll at a private college or university, and 85 percent intended to enroll at a four-year institution.

Assembling cheat sheets for each of these popular institutions was very doable. The goal of the summary documents was to provide advisors and students with a single-page document summarizing the key summer steps that they needed to complete. For each task, an institution-specific cheat sheet provided associated deadlines as well as the relevant web pages and phone numbers should students need more information or additional support. The documents were to serve as a guide for advisors but also be sufficiently straightforward that students could follow them as well.

Putting together these cheat sheets was an illuminating exercise in its own right. The data was fairly easy to assemble—nearly all that students needed to know about required summer tasks was available online. Rarely, if ever, was it necessary to call an institution to get additional information. Furthermore, at least 80 percent of the needed details were contained on web pages specifically designed for admitted students. But for just about every institution, some of the material that students needed was located on other web pages. For instance, the admitted students' page might state that students need to take academic placement tests, but details about how and when to register for the tests would be located on a separate page (not always linked to the admitted students' page). Having defined what each cheat sheet should include, assembling all of the relevant summer information for a single institution took about an hour. This was after developing a sense of the details that each cheat sheet needed to include. You can imagine how this search and discovery process might be substantially more challenging and discouraging for a first-generation college-intending student, especially one who has only intermittent Internet access during the summer and doesn't know what information to search for in the first place.

The goal of all these materials and structures was to help advisors identify obstacles to successful matriculation and to work with students to develop and carry out concrete plans to resolve them. After meeting with a student once, the advisor would follow up with the student regularly and meet again in person as needed. For students who seemed well on the way to college in the first meeting, advisors might follow up only once or twice during the summer. But they would reach out more often to students whose postsecondary plans seemed more at risk during the initial assessment.

IMPLEMENTING SUMMER COLLEGE CONNECT

As with our efforts to document the extent of summer melt among students served by uAspire, we once again relied on the Last Dollar Scholarship applicants to identify the college-intending recent Boston Public Schools graduates to whom advisors would reach out. These students had been accepted to college, applied for financial aid, worked with uAspire during the academic year, and by the end of high school had decided where they planned to enroll. uAspire advisors promoted the scholarship program across the Boston public high schools and with the students they counseled in those schools throughout the year. uAspire was able to collect nearly a thousand applications for the scholarship from the class of 2011 graduates, a considerably higher number of applicants than in previous years.

This led to an unexpected challenge as well as an opportunity. uAspire did not have enough advisors to provide summer outreach to all of the Last Dollar Scholarship applicants. In fact, Cox felt that they could provide high-quality services to slightly less than half. One option would have been to target specific groups of students, such as those with high levels of unmet financial need. The truth was, however, that we lacked solid evidence regarding which students were likely to benefit. Advisors reasoned that few of the students they served were impervious to potential barriers that arose over the summer. They knew neither which students would be most responsive nor which would stand to benefit the most from summer support.

Still, faced with limited resources and more eligible students than uAspire could serve, a decision had to be made about which students to prioritize. One possibility was to make an educated guess about which students would benefit the most from summer outreach and define selection criteria based on this reasoning. Another possibility was to do just the opposite—select a pool of students to receive summer outreach and support completely at random. For student-serving organizations, the notion of randomly rather than purposefully targeting students for additional support may seem foreign or even counter to the goals and mission that undergird their work.

While both approaches have their merits, our proposal to Giannino-Racine and Cox was to use a lottery to randomly determine who received outreach. In making this proposal, we highlighted several advantages of a lottery-based approach: First, lottery-based selection was equitable in that it gave every eligible student an equal chance of receiving outreach. Second, using a lottery could also support uAspire's future fundraising and advocacy efforts by providing rigorous evidence of the impact of Summer College Connect on subsequent college outcomes. Because all students had an equal chance of being selected, those whose names were pulled out of the hat would be just like the group of students not selected for outreach. More concretely, both groups would have the same average unmet financial need, the same share of males, the same average high school GPA, and so on. They would differ only in that one group would get advisor outreach during the summer. Therefore, uAspire could make a strong case that any improvements in students' college outcomes as a result of Summer College Connect were due entirely to the program, rather than any of the multitude of factors that influence whether students enter and succeed in college. Finally, the lottery-based approach would allow us to answer the question that we had been wrestling with since the Providence pilot program: Would a more mainstream population of students benefit from proactive summer support? If we found positive impacts from a larger-scale summer melt experiment in Boston, it would strengthen the argument that policy makers and other educators should provide students with college counseling during the summer after high school.

Giannino-Racine and Cox engaged in serious conversations regarding the proposed lottery-based approach and ultimately signed off on using it as the mechanism for identifying which students would receive advisor outreach. We then turned our attention to securing buy-in from uAspire's frontline advisors, an equally (or likely even more important) group of stakeholders who needed to be on board with the lottery plan. After all, this would require them to withhold outreach from certain students with whom they had worked during the prior year, with whom they may have had a strong relationship, and whom the advisors thought could benefit from their support over the summer. If the advisors did not buy into the idea of using a lottery, the potential for a rigorous evaluation of the impact of Summer College Connect would be diminished.

Through the SCC design process, we had developed close relationships with the uAspire advisors. Still, the advisors had no previous experience with a lottery approach to research within the context of their work, and needed the space to process this philosophical shift in determining which students received organizational outreach. Cox stepped in to lead the discussion. In a meeting with the advisors, she outlined the rationale for using a lottery to select students, emphasizing issues of equity and the potential long-term benefits to uAspire. She also articulated what became a final governing principle of SCC: any student uAspire had worked with during the year could reach out to an advisor for support. Regardless of whether they were chosen to receive outreach, the expectation was that advisors would provide high-quality support to any student who initiated contact. The distinction between the two groups in the lottery, therefore, was not which had access to advising after high school graduation but rather which students received additional outreach from an advisor during the summer.

After Cox framed the issue for the participating advisors, she gave them the opportunity to pose any questions or express any reservations. What ensued was a transparent, thoughtful, and honest discussion that helped to strengthen the overall design of the intervention, allowed us as researchers to become more attuned to the practitioner context, and set the stage for open communication that would continue through the life of the project. Cox then asked that advisors go around the room and, one by one, express buy-in to the research design and a commitment to maintain fidelity to the lottery assignments. As young researchers, it was a powerful experience to observe Cox facilitate this meeting and to hear each advisor commit to the project. It has been equally powerful to observe in the years following Summer College Connect that uAspire has adopted lottery-based investigations as a regular feature of its efforts to assess the impact of its programming.

Applicants to uAspire's Last Dollar Scholarship were primarily from low-income families and were primarily students of color.

From this pool, we collaborated with Alex Chewning, uAspire's director of research and evaluation, to identify a random subset of students to receive outreach and assign them to advisors. Eleven advisors staffed the SCC outreach. Depending on their availability for SCC balanced with other summer commitments, caseloads ranged from ten to forty-seven students per advisor. Where possible, advisors served students with whom they worked during the academic year in order to capitalize on existing personal connections. Just as students were walking across the graduation stage to receive their diploma, Summer College Connect was ready to launch.

LAUNCH AND IMPACT OF SUMMER COLLEGE CONNECT

Advisors began reaching out to students at the end of June. Given all the time invested to design and prepare for Summer College Connect, there was a collective hope that throngs of students would be pouring through the doors to meet with advisors. Instead, the summer started with only a slow trickle of meetings. One challenge advisors faced was simply getting in touch with students. They would call the number on file and leave a message but not hear back. They would send e-mails to students but get no response or receive a bounce-back message. In other cases, advisors would make contact over the phone and invite a student in for a meeting. However, students were often reluctant to make the trip, either because they had to travel from the outlying neighborhood where they lived, or because the meeting was in an unfamiliar setting. Students were accustomed to meeting with their advisor in their own high school, and prior to the summer, few had firsthand experience visiting uAspire's downtown location, nestled within a large office building in Boston's city center. In fact, uAspire advisors shared stories of SCC students getting as close as the subway stop just blocks from their office, only to turn around after being unable to locate the office or having forgotten a photo ID, which was required to enter the building. For these and other reasons, many students would schedule an appointment with an advisor only to be a no-show or reschedule at the last moment. By mid-July, only a couple dozen students had met with an advisor, and concern and doubt set in: Had all of the SCC planning been for naught?

Several weeks into the intervention, this concern spurred a brainstorming session to discuss how to increase student response rates. One strategy was to shift away from phone and e-mail to communication methods that were more popular among students. Several of the advisors started reaching out via text and reported substantially greater success in making contact with students. Facebook also held promise. In a burst of inspiration, Cox devised Mo' Money, uAspire's SCC Facebook persona. As with text messaging, reaching out via Mo' Money proved to be a more successful means of contacting students. A third strategy was for advisors to meet students somewhere in their neighborhood rather than at the uAspire office. Students were responsive to this offer since it meant they did not have to navigate the trip to uAspire's downtown location, could meet with an advisor on a lunch break, and did not have to miss work, family, or social commitments. With these three strategies, advisors increased their focus on meeting students where they were, literally or figuratively: texting on their phones, messaging and chatting on Facebook, or in person in students' own neighborhoods. Finally, as the saying goes, time is often the best remedy. Student responsiveness picked up, particularly toward the end of July, around the time that they received their first tuition bills.

The uAspire advisors now had a steady flow of students visiting their office for one-on-one meetings. Students arrived, often with a stack of college paperwork in hand and a friend or parent in tow. Dressed in casual summer clothing or wearing uniforms from summer day jobs, the students brought a wide range of questions, concerns, hopes, and goals. Some of them were visibly enthusiastic about their college plans, speaking rapidly about their new roommate assignment or recent experiences at orientation. Others were more subdued and expressed concern that their college plans might yet fall through or confusion about a communication from the college that was filled with unfamiliar technical jargon.

Advisors were struck by the observation that, despite the diversity in student characteristics, in terms of both their academic records and their postsecondary plans, all of the students with whom they met faced at least one barrier to enrollment over the summer. As one advisor reflected, "We reached a TON of students through SCC! I really didn't anticipate how much students didn't know—many students were surprised they had forms to fill out during summer, or that they had a bill. This work is such a big win for us and our students."

In fact, more often than not, students faced multiple barriers, many of which they and their families did not anticipate. For example, on more than one occasion, students did not realize until they met with an advisor that payment for the fall semester would be due during the summer. Even more commonly, many students' limited Internet access over the summer meant they had not yet logged on to their online college accounts or realized the importance of doing so. Checking e-mail for the first time during a summer meeting with an advisor often revealed a host of unread messages and overdue tasks—from registering for housing to completing entrance loan counseling to waiving health insurance— that were urgently awaiting their attention and that, if left undone, threatened to delay or prevent their enrollment. Despite the initial challenges, advisors were gratified by the work that they were able to do over the summer.

Notably, advisors regularly reflected on the fact that students who seemed "all set" (proactive, organized, accepted into school) at the end of high school were in need of considerable help navigating their final steps to enrollment. Further, students were extremely grateful for the meetings, even when those meetings brought to light difficult situations and conversations.

The themes and principles that guided the planning of Summer College Connect reverberated in advisors' interactions with students and their families during that summer. Reflecting on their role as guide in student and family decision making, advisors shared poignant moments of mediating interactions between parents and students when communication broke down in the face of disagreements and stress related to college financing. In one case, a parent and student came to meet with an advisor together, even though they were not on speaking terms. The tuition bill had just been issued. The student was worried that her public college was unaffordable and wanted to find a cheaper option, while the mother insisted that the student was overlooking the bigger picture. The uAspire advisor took care to speak with both the student and her mother individually before facilitating a joint meeting. Through a ninety-minute session, the advisor, student, and parent ultimately were able to agree on two viable options, articulate the financial ramifications of each, and identify next steps.

Some advising moments took the shape of small yet meaningful assistance. One proactive mother had confused the subsidized and unsubsidized loans on her daughter's financial aid award. Thinking that the subsidized portion was the loan that accrued interest while the student was in school, she and the student had declined the full subsidized loan while accepting the full unsubsidized loan—a misstep that the college financial aid office would not necessarily catch, yet one with meaningful implications for the family. When the student and parent realized the mistake during a summer advising meeting, they feared that the process could not be undone, but were able to rectify the situation once the advisor explained how a change could be made in writing in advance of loan disbursement. Another student had a limited relationship with her father but wanted to take him up on his offer to help her pay her first tuition bill. The student was overwhelmed by the process and wanted to better understand the payment plan in order to explain it to her father. The advisor sat with the student to navigate the payment plan information online together. Then the student and advisor, together, called the father to discuss options.

Perhaps due to uAspire's substantive focus on college financing and affordability, the primary support that students received over the summer related to financial aid. Students sought help to better understand their financial aid packages and tuition bills, to lobby for more financial aid, and to set up tuition payment plans, among other aid-related tasks. In addition, advisors helped students navigate nuanced processes and avoid common pitfalls. For example, advisors estimated that they helped the students as a group save tens of thousands of dollars by guiding them through the steps required to waive unnecessary fees, such as student health insurance, that appeared on their tuition bills by default, in accordance with Massachusetts state law. In addition, advisors advised students with generous financial aid packages that they could actually decline unnecessary loans and save a few thousand dollars of borrowing. They helped other students explore the option of commuting to school from home when the costs of living on campus made college unaffordable. Finally, advisors provided smaller tips related to things like renting or purchasing used books. In these ways, advisors were helping students not only to start, but to "start smart" in their college careers.

Equally important, advisors cultivated in their students the skills and confidence to handle college-related tasks and processes more independently in the future. For example, one advisor recounted working with a student who needed to call a financial aid officer at her intended college to discuss a possible appeal to her financial aid package. Prior to the call, the advisor coached the student on how to conduct the call, practicing what to say and how to say it. The student then dialed the phone with poise and confidence—which dissolved the instant the financial aid office answered the call. The student literally threw the phone at her advisor, pleading to her to conduct the call on her behalf. The advisor handed the phone back to the student, firmly encouraging her to handle the call on her own while the advisor stood by for support.

Advisors wrestled with the question of how often they should be reaching out to students to offer support and coaching—where is the line, they asked, between actively encouraging students and chasing after them? Advisors also confronted the reality that their work may have led to instances of summer melt—those cases where reconsidering college plans was not necessarily a bad thing. For some students, the serious financial implications of their post-secondary plans had flown quietly under the radar until summer meetings with advisors and looming tuition bills revealed plans that were financially untenable. High school seniors often viewed "making college plans" as getting *accepted* to an institution, not figuring out how to afford it. Students sometimes expressed a belief that if they were accepted at a given school, the finances would inevitably "work out in the end." In this context, advisors navigated difficult conversations to communicate the financial implications of college plans months after the student had become attached to the idea of attending a particular institution. One advisor, for example, described her role as "dream crusher" when she challenged students to recognize that their decision to attend a particular school was putting them at substantial risk financially. For some of these students, the summer meeting with an advisor marked the first time they had fully explored the financial implications of their college plans.

Some of these students had sensed there might be a problem with finances, but had avoided the topic with family and with themselves, committed to achieving their goal of college attendance "no matter the cost." For example, one advisor recounted working with a student who was determined to attend an expensive, low-selectivity private college despite facing a $17,000 gap between the cost of attendance and her financial aid package. Her family did not have the funds to pay the tuition deposit, let alone the first tuition bill. In addition, the family did not have the credit history needed to obtain private loans. Although the advisor encouraged the student to consider alternative postsecondary plans, the student proceeded to solicit assistance more broadly, asking friends and extended family to cosign loans with her. Finally, a cousin agreed, and she was able to take out a private loan for the necessary tuition dollars. Advisors ended the summer worried that this approach to college financing would not be sustainable beyond the student's freshman year.

To examine the impact of Summer College Connect on student outcomes, we connected several data sources: uAspire data on students' background characteristics; advisors' logs from their interactions with students over the summer; and college enrollment and persistence data from the National Student Clearinghouse. With this combined data, we were able to learn the extent to which students had responded to advisors' outreach and whether the advisors' support had generated meaningful improvements in students' college outcomes. The results were at once surprising and edifying. Advisors reached out to all of those assigned to receive support, just over four hundred students, and had substantive communications (via phone, text, or Facebook) with more than three-quarters of them. In these communications, advisors checked in with students about the status of their college plans, offering discrete encouragement or advice or receiving reassurance that the student's college plans were truly all set. Advisors had at least one in-depth, typically in-person, meeting with more than half of the students. In contrast, of the students not selected for outreach, virtually none interacted with uAspire during the summer. All of these students had been reminded at the start of the summer that they could seek support from uAspire over the summer months. That so few of these students sought help is a strong signal that students stand to benefit from more active encouragement to take up support resources over the summer.

Students who received outreach from an advisor were approximately five percentage points more likely to enroll immediately in college than students who did not receive proactive outreach—83 percent versus 78 percent (see figure 4.1). To put this margin into perspective, consider that the financial aid research has consistently found that $1,000 in additional grant aid increases enrollment by three to six percentage points. Summer College Connect increased enrollment by the same margin but at a cost of only $200 per student. Another way to interpret the size of this effect is that SCC alleviated nearly one-quarter of the summer melt among uAspire students.[1] Of even greater importance, as

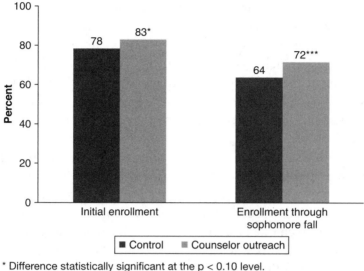

Figure 4.1. Share of students who initially enroll in college and who enroll continuously through sophomore fall

figure 4.1 also shows, students who received outreach were nearly eight percentage points more likely to persist into the sophomore year of college (as far out as we have been able to observe them at the time of writing this book). For both enrollment and persistence, the effects of SCC were largest for the lowest-income uAspire students. For example, among the lowest-income students, outreach increased immediate college enrollment from 76 percent to almost 89 percent.[2] Among these students, those receiving outreach were also thirteen percentage points more likely to remain enrolled into their sophomore year.

Among higher-income students, the summer outreach actually had a negative impact on initial college enrollment.[3] While this result may seem puzzling, the data revealed that these were also students who faced the largest gaps between their financial aid and the cost of attendance—potentially a significant financial hardship. That initial enrollment declined for these students was consistent with uAspire's philosophical stance that not all summer melt is bad. In fact, three semesters later, these students were equally likely (compared to their similarly higher-income counterparts who did not receive outreach) to be enrolled in college but were far less likely to be at their originally intended college. In short, these students may have benefited from uAspire's advice to delay enrollment and find an alternative college that represented a better financial decision.

The substantial impact of advisor outreach on students' college persistence supports the earlier statement that students' struggles with summer obstacles to enrollment do not indicate their potential for collegiate success. With help overcoming these financial and procedural challenges, students were able to succeed in college. These positive results also seem to validate the uAspire advisors' approach of building students' capacity to handle summer challenges independently rather than completing the tasks for the students. With the skills and strategies they developed over the summer, students may have had greater confidence to navigate similar hurdles during freshman year (like renewing their FAFSA) and to complete required tasks during the following summer. Based on the success of this initial implementation of Summer College Connect, uAspire has continued to experiment with summer outreach, as discussed in the next two chapters.

SCHOOL DISTRICT–LED COUNSELOR OUTREACH

The positive impacts of Summer College Connect confirmed that proactive summer support is beneficial not only in a unique educational setting like the Met but also for a more mainstream population of students. Yet in many ways, uAspire is also unique. Though it serves students attending mainstream urban, public schools, uAspire is a high-functioning nonprofit organization that does not face many of the structural challenges encountered by public school systems.

While in an ideal policy landscape every community would have such organizations, a broad scaling of summer college counseling could not expect to rely on organizations like uAspire. As exciting as the uAspire results were, it remained an open question whether summer outreach would be feasible and effective if implemented directly by a large, mainstream school district. The remainder of this chapter addresses this question by discussing the success of summer college-going interventions implemented by two large U.S. school districts, one in Georgia and one in Texas. These districts' efforts provide important evidence that summer outreach efforts can be successfully implemented by public school systems throughout the country. We learned of these districts through our connection to the Strategic Data Project (SDP) at Harvard University.

At the same time that we were developing the summer melt intervention with uAspire, work led by the SDP was uncovering high rates of summer melt in two other areas of the country—Fulton County, Georgia, and Fort Worth, Texas. The Strategic Data Project is a partnership project between education policy researchers at Harvard University and educational agencies around the country. The mission of SDP is to transform the use of data in education to improve student achievement. One of the strategies SDP employs in working toward this mission is to conduct "diagnostics" or deep descriptive analyses based on data held by each partner agency. One of the SDP diagnostics is particularly focused on students' preparation for and success in transitioning to and through college. A second SDP strategy is to place high-skilled data analysts in each partner agency for a two-year fellowship. SDP fellows are recruited through a national search process and are intended to help grow partner agencies' capacity to use data and analysis to inform decision making.

Building on our work to assess the extent of summer melt nationally and in Boston, Strategic Data Project fellows in the Fulton County Schools, Korynn Schooley and Niveen Vosler, and in the Fort Worth Independent School District, Lindsay Daugherty, were investigating summer melt within their districts. The SDP college-going diagnostics provided these districts with new information about the actual college enrollment patterns of their high school graduates. As with other agencies that learn about summer melt for the first time, both districts were quite surprised by the SDP findings. Their college-going rates were far lower than what counselors expected based on their understanding of students' postsecondary plans. Of the college-intending students, more than one in five in Fulton and two in five in Fort Worth failed to enroll in the year following high school, with rates of summer melt even higher among the lowest-income students in both districts. The districts were spurred into action by these high rates of summer melt. At the same time that we were devising Summer College Connect, Schooley, Chris Matthews, Fulton's executive director of student support services at the time, and others were leading the development of Summer PACE (Personalized Assistance for College Enrollment) in Fulton County; and Lindsay Daugherty was building Summer Link in Fort Worth.[4]

Summer PACE (Fulton County Schools)

Schooley and colleagues recruited counselors in six district schools to staff Summer PACE. Unlike the uAspire advisors who were employed for twelve months, the participating Fulton counselors were typically off contract in the summer months. Therefore, an important implementation detail was identifying additional funding to compensate counselors for their time during the summer. The district was able to do so through a combination of grant funding and a flexible reappropriation of its operating budget. As in the Met intervention, the Fulton counselors provided outreach to students who had just graduated from the high schools in which they worked. Unlike the uAspire advisors, the Fulton counselors were not well equipped to handle issues related to college financial aid. Therefore, Schooley and others organized training on various financial aid topics, such as the FAFSA and Georgia's merit-based scholarship program. Counselors conducted outreach from early June through late July and used a variety of outreach strategies such as phone, e-mail, text, Facebook, and Twitter to reach students and offer summer college-going support.

As with Summer College Connect, Schooley and others implemented Summer PACE in the context of a lottery-based study that allowed them to assess the impact of the intervention on college enrollment outcomes. In each of the six participating schools, eighty students were selected to receive outreach from one of two counselors. The Fulton results are surprisingly consistent with those from uAspire, particularly with respect to students from low-income backgrounds. In Fulton, low-income status was identified based on students' qualification for free- or reduced-price school meals (FRL). Just over one-third of students who were eligible for Summer PACE, by virtue of having applied and gotten accepted to college and reported intentions to enroll, were also FRL eligible. While Summer PACE had no impact on the non-FRL students, 93 percent of whom enrolled on time regardless of the intervention, it had a particularly large impact on timely enrollment for students who did qualify for FRL. For these students, summer counselor-led outreach and support increased on-time college enrollment from 63 percent to 72 percent. This was still far below the on-time enrollment rate for the financially better-off students in the study, but it substantially reduced the differential in enrollment. As with uAspire, Fulton has continued to offer the Summer PACE outreach since this initial summer.

Summer Link (Fort Worth Independent School District)

In Fort Worth, all district high schools were provided with the option to implement Summer Link, and all but two took the opportunity. Different from the programs in Boston and Fulton County, Summer Link was staffed by a broader array of district personnel, including counselors, teachers, and other school staff, and sought to reach all college-intending recent graduates, rather than a randomly selected subset of students. Therefore, Link provides a useful test case for comprehensive implementation of a summer outreach intervention.

In Fort Worth, participating schools were required to provide financial support for summer staff from their own operating budgets. The cost of Summer Link was approximately $48 per student. Similar to the other sites, Summer Link staff provided a variety of supports to students. These included reviewing with students the steps they needed to take to matriculate, helping with FAFSA completion and other college-related paperwork, and providing social and emotional support related to the transition to college. Also similar to the other sites, participating students most commonly sought guidance related to financial aid.[5]

Because Summer Link was implemented essentially as a whole-district effort, it was more challenging, methodologically speaking (than with a lottery-based study) to isolate the unique impact of the intervention on students' enrollment outcomes. Yet, a comparison with the previous cohort of seniors revealed a five percentage point positive difference in the rate of timely college matriculation, overall, with year-over-year improvements of a larger magnitude in certain schools. Positive feedback from participating staff members also suggested the success of the Summer Link program. As one Fort Worth staff member wrote, "Thank you for the opportunity to help with Summer Link. I really enjoyed this experience . . . due to [the fact] that I usually work with the students from a negative truancy standpoint, this was a refreshing time to work with the students in a more positive light."

In sum, the available evidence suggests that both the Summer PACE and Summer Link programs yielded positive returns for participating students in terms of mitigating summer melt by a significant margin. Together with uAspire's Summer College Connect, these three programs add to the evidence that students are responsive to and receive benefits from summer outreach and support. Importantly, Summer PACE and Summer Link serve as proof positive that large school systems, along with smaller and sometimes more nimble nonprofit organizations, have the potential to successfully implement summer outreach initiatives to address summer melt.

CHAPTER 5

◆ ◆ ◆

Ten Texts to College
Using Technology to "Nudge" Students

The increasing attention to the summer after high school as an important time in students' transition to college was not limited to Boston, Fulton County, Georgia, or Fort Worth, Texas. Educators in other parts of the country were also taking up the charge of actively reaching out to and supporting students during the summer months. For example, College Bound and St. Louis Graduates, both in St. Louis, Missouri; On Point for College in Syracuse, New York; and Career Beginnings in Hartford, Connecticut, provided students with high-quality, comprehensive counseling support beginning in high school and continuing through (and often after) the first day of college. The rising interest in summer melt brought with it new questions about the best ways to guide students through this turbulent period.

First, to whose offer of help are students most responsive? Most typically, school-based counselors and community-based financial aid advisors provided outreach to students. For a variety of reasons, this approach is both sensible and practical. In many cases, the counselors and advisors had personal relationships with the students they were contacting. In addition, they were experts in counseling, financial aid, or both, and so could provide informed guidance and were well-positioned to respond to unexpected challenges or circumstances that arose.

And yet, though student responsiveness to summer outreach in Boston and Fulton County was impressive, there was nonetheless room for improvement. While uAspire advisors were able to have some level of phone or e-mail dialogue with 75 percent of the students to whom they reached out, only about half of the students actually met with an advisor during the summer to review their college plans. In Fulton County, only three in ten students who received outreach communicated with a counselor. And while interaction rates were higher among low-income students in Fulton, even among this group, four in ten did not communicate with a counselor over the summer. In both sites, even for the students with whom counselors did communicate, getting in touch with the students took a substantial amount of time and effort. Counselors often had to make repeated phone calls or send several messages before connecting with a student.

The difficulty in contacting students may have stemmed from the counselors' modes of outreach. Either because they lacked more complete contact information or because of how they were accustomed to communicating with students, most counselors and advisors initially resorted to e-mail and phone. Over the past several years, however, we have found that many students check their e-mail with decreasing frequency. And when they do, it's unlikely that a counselor's message stands out from the volume of personal communication, school correspondence, and spam filling their in-boxes. Reaching students by phone also tends to bear little fruit. Students rarely picked up when counselors called, either because they were busy or were screening an unfamiliar number. In other cases, students did not have their voicemail set up or their numbers were disconnected or had changed. Even when counselors were able to leave a voicemail, students often did not return their calls.

Another impediment to higher take-up rates of summer support may have been the time of day that counselors typically reached out. During the summer, many counselors preferred to work in the morning and early afternoon to accommodate child care schedules or simply to have afternoons off. Unfortunately, the students were typically working or asleep during these periods. What sometimes ensued was a back-and-forth game of phone tag in which a student might engage for a few days, only to eventually lose interest in connecting with a school counselor.

Another question is how to most effectively provide outreach, information, and support to students at scale. Summer counseling initiatives are inexpensive compared to other strategies that policy makers have employed to increase college access among low-income students. As noted in chapter 4, research on financial aid has consistently found that $1,000 in additional grant aid increases college enrollment by three to six percentage points. The summer counseling interventions in Boston, Fulton, and Fort Worth generated enrollment increases of a similar margin for a fraction of the cost. Nonetheless, even counselor-led outreach may not be scalable in resourced-constrained settings. Each counselor hired to conduct outreach was compensated approximately $4,000 for the summer and had a caseload of anywhere from thirty to fifty students, resulting in a cost per district of tens of thousands of dollars. For the superintendent of a large school district, providing summer outreach to all college-intending, low-income high school graduates could run well over $100,000. An investment of an additional $150 per college-bound graduate may be small relative to a district's overall budget. Yet an expenditure of this size may be infeasible given district budget constraints and cutbacks, even where college-intending students may stand to benefit substantially from the outreach.

THE PROMISE OF TEXT MESSAGING

Given the promise of summer outreach and the problem of constrained resources, one potential solution is to engage students via messaging technology instead of direct outreach from counselors. uAspire's work with students supported this possibility. The logs of the uAspire advisors' summer interactions with students revealed an interesting pattern: a substantial number of students were unresponsive to outreach by phone and e-mail, even after advisors made multiple attempts to contact them. But many of these same students were very responsive once advisors switched to text or Facebook messaging.

This change was unsurprising. The counselors who staffed the original intervention in Providence indicated these were the most effective modes of communication for reaching students. Early on in the Providence pilot, the counselors realized that students who gave nothing but radio silence to their phone calls would respond to text and Facebook outreach within seconds of when the counselor typed the message. Students' responsiveness to text messages probably resonates if you have teenage children of your own or work with adolescents. Most likely, text messaging is the best way to communicate with them—and the way that they most frequently interact with each other.

Might it be more effective to build a summer outreach campaign around text or Facebook messaging? After all, there are really three major aspects of what the counselors were achieving in their outreach: (1) informing students about tasks they might not be aware of; (2) reminding students about task- and college-specific deadlines; and (3) helping students complete these complex steps. Text or Facebook messaging can accomplish the first two goals, and facilitate the third by getting through to students who don't respond to phone and e-mail outreach. These strategies require relatively little information to generate highly personalized messages and disseminate them to a large number of students. Students need to provide just their name, cell number or Facebook user name, and intended college. Another advantage of this approach is that most college-intending students from a given district plan to attend one of a fairly small number of colleges. Therefore, assembling the college-specific task and due date information for the relevant set of colleges and universities is a manageable task. All that is needed is a way to deliver the right message to the right student at the appropriate time during the summer.

One possibility is to deliver messages via Facebook. There are several advantages to using the social network platform. First, it precludes having to collect students' cell phone numbers. Counselors can look up students using the Facebook search tools, and if students accept a "friend" request, counselors can send them messages or chat with them online. Facebook has the added advantage of free message delivery and receipt. Finally, Facebook has the potential to influence the enrollment decisions not only of the targeted students but also others in these students' networks. For instance, if messages successfully lead a student to attend orientation at her intended college, she might post about the experience on her Facebook page. Other students who see these posts might in turn be induced to attend orientation if they haven't already. The power of Facebook to generate this type of social influence on desirable behaviors has been demonstrated in other policy arenas, such as whether individuals vote on election day.[1]

And yet, there are several limitations to using Facebook for message delivery. First, Facebook allows organizations to have pages that other people can "like," but restricts organizations from "friending" other Facebook users. So to generate friend requests, and thereby deliver individual messages to students, counselors must use their individual accounts. In addition, it is difficult to automate message delivery with Facebook. If, after students accepted a friend request, they agreed to join a Facebook group (e.g. UMass-Boston class of 2014), a counselor could deliver messages to the entire group. But even students who agree to be friends with a counselor or advisor may not respond to invitations to join such groups. For these students, counselors would have to send the same message individually to each student with whom they were friends, limiting the potential of Facebook for large-scale, automated outreach. Another obstacle is that many schools and districts restrict their counselors from using Facebook to communicate with students. Finally, counselors may prefer not to give students access to their personal Facebook page.

By comparison, text messaging offers many of the same benefits of Facebook without the prohibitive limitations. Texting is the primary way that young people communicate with each other.[2] Even among the lowest-income families, most teenagers have cell phones, and nearly all of them use text messaging. Further, many teens with cell phones have plans that allow for unlimited text messaging. It would be possible to reach as many, if not more, students as through Facebook, and importantly, students wouldn't need access to a networked computer or a smartphone to receive outreach. Because text messaging is such a common mode of communication among teenagers, messages might also make it easier for students to connect with an advisor for assistance during the summer. Whereas students may be unlikely to return a phone call or walk into a school office to schedule a meeting, requesting help via text message requires only a minimal investment. All students have to do is send a quick reply to a message they received. Text messages could also conceivably be automated to send the same message to many students at once, using tools like Google Voice and GroupMe.

A text messaging campaign would also build on growing evidence in the field of behavioral economics demonstrating the power of prompts to positively influence individual decision making. Using ideas popularized by Richard Thaler and Cass Sunstein's book *Nudge*, researchers have already applied behavioral economic strategies to achieve a range of socially desirable outcomes, such as increasing the rates with which individuals contribute to financial savings accounts or get flu vaccines.[3] As these studies demonstrate, text messages can effectively prompt people to deal with a task in the moment, before their attention is diverted elsewhere. This is certainly relevant to the summer after high school when students have to complete several discrete tasks yet face a variety of distractions, from attractive diversions like spending time with friends to more pressing commitments like work or family responsibilities (such as those of the students profiled in chapters 2 and 3).

In addition, text messaging holds promise for more than simply providing task-specific prompts. For students who have smartphones and data plans (a rapidly growing segment of all cell phone users), messages could include college- and task-specific web links, enabling students to complete many tasks right from their mobile phones. Given the impulsiveness of teenagers and the pleasure of instant gratification, putting task completion literally at students' fingertips could prove to be particularly impactful. The behavioral economics literature has also illustrated how overly complex information (for example, about retirement savings) can lead people to put off decisions indefinitely.[4] Text messaging provides a means of sending students digestible, consolidated, and timely bursts of information about the tasks they need to complete in order to successfully matriculate. This stepwise approach might be more effective than most colleges' usual strategy of sending one comprehensive and often complicated list of all the matriculation tasks students must complete over the summer.

Despite the potential benefits of text messaging, this strategy is not without its challenges. The first hurdle is how to collect students' cell phone numbers. High school exit surveys conducted by some districts provide a natural opportunity for gathering this information. These surveys also provide data regarding whether and where students are planning to enroll in college. In theory, by adding an additional field to the survey, it would be possible to request and collect students' cell numbers. This strategy works for school districts that are willing to (or already do) administer exit surveys.

Another challenge to utilizing text messaging as a communication method is whether school districts (or educational agencies more broadly) are willing and able to serve as the ostensible sender of text messages to recent high school graduates. While school districts routinely send students and families e-mail and postal correspondence—and in numerous settings even use "robo-calling" to deliver messages—districts have not typically communicated via text messaging. Would the district legal offices determine that they had the authority to send text messages to students? Would student and/or parent consent be required?

These questions stem from the fact that, unlike postal mail or e-mail, sending text messages potentially imposes costs on the intended recipient. This would not be an issue for students with unlimited texting plans, but for those who "pay as you go," each message would incur a small charge. While the cost would be on the order of a dime per message, charges associated with a summer's worth of messages could add up, and moreover, the cost per message might escalate if students exceed a cap on their monthly text message plan.

Based on the challenges discussed here, we identified several principles to inform the design of a summer college-transition text messaging campaign. First, partner agencies would message only those students who voluntarily provided their cell phone numbers. Second, outreach would be limited to ten messages total throughout the summer. If the average "pay as you go" customer is charged ten cents per message, this would cap out-of-pocket expenses at a dollar per student. Finally, if a student asked not to receive text messages, delivery of all future messages would immediately be canceled.

MOVING FROM PROMISE TO IMPLEMENTATION

These guidelines collectively became the general parameters for one component of a broader set of interventions we called Project SCOPE (Summer Counselor Outreach for Postsecondary Education). We referred to the text intervention as SCOPE-Digital.

Several organizations joined us in implementing SCOPE-Digital. uAspire was again a key partner, not only in Boston but also in its Lawrence and Springfield, Massachusetts, sites. Adding these cities into the mix offered a valuable opportunity. Boston is unique among urban areas in its concentration of high-quality college-access programs as well as the priority that both city politicians, like former mayor Thomas Menino, and local organizations, like the Private Industry Council, have placed on increasing college going among city residents. Including Lawrence and Springfield as intervention sites enabled us to examine how the information and prompts provided by text messages would impact students residing in areas that offered little access to college-planning supports or information.

But our ability to generalize about the efficacy of a text messaging campaign to reduce summer melt would be limited if results were based exclusively on implementing the intervention with uAspire, an organization with deep expertise in financial aid and college affordability. Therefore, including traditional school districts as partners was key to generating evidence of the broader feasibility and impact of text messaging as an intervention strategy. As a result of an ongoing research collaboration with Eric Bettinger (Stanford University), Bridget Terry Long (Harvard University), and Laura Owen (San Diego State University), and Owen's strong district relationships, the Dallas Independent School District (Dallas ISD) and the Denver Public Schools signed on to partner in implementing the summer text campaign.

Messaging at Scale

We briefly considered simply sending the messages ourselves or training counselors to batch messages with a tool like Google Voice. Peter Bergman of Columbia University had used this approach in a text messaging intervention to provide parents of middle and high school students with information about their child's missing assignments, grades, and upcoming tests.[5] But there were thousands of potential recipients across the sites. Sending messages manually would be cumbersome and labor intensive, making it unlikely that this approach would be scalable beyond this intervention.

Once again, we benefited considerably from Owen's connections. Specifically, she had learned about two Johns Hopkins medical school students, Michael Lin and Ralph Passarella, who had created a text messaging platform to assist with clinical trials: imagine medical researchers testing the efficacy of a new asthma medication and wanting to ensure that patients complied with their medication schedule. Lin and Passarella founded a startup, Signal Vine, to provide services such as sending automated text message reminders to patients to take their medicine.[6] The messages could be customized to each patient's unique schedule and could include other personalized information that the researchers wanted to convey.

Lin and Passarella had little experience working in education and, at the time, no plans to expand into the education sector. But they were entrepreneurial, thoughtful, and nimble, and were interested in the concept for the summer melt text campaign. They were also eager for an opportunity to grow their fledgling business. An additional benefit of their experience in the health sector is that their system complied with federal regulations for working with sensitive individual information.

The Signal Vine platform could automate message delivery exactly in the way we had hoped. To create and distribute the messages, Signal Vine required two separate spreadsheets. The first would contain each student's name, cell phone number, and a numeric ID corresponding to the student's intended college. The second spreadsheet would contain institution-specific information on the tasks incoming students had to complete in the months prior to matriculation as well as the due dates and web links relevant to those tasks. The Signal Vine system would stitch these two spreadsheets together and automatically deliver the right content to the right student on a predetermined schedule. The system could deliver messages at any time of day, which avoided the issue of counselors conducting outreach during hours when students were unlikely to be available. Further, Lin and Passarella could configure the system so that if a student wrote back requesting help, an administrator could generate an e-mail to a local counselor assigned to that student, notifying the counselor that the student requested assistance and providing the student's name and phone number.

To construct each task reminder, the Signal Vine system would insert student- and task-specific information into message templates. These templates had to be written like Mad Libs— language common across all students was interspersed with blank fields to be populated with the individualized information collected from students and their intended college. Each template had to be capped at 160 characters—the length of one text message. Some of the messages contained reminders about discrete tasks, like registering for orientation. Other messages encouraged students to seek assistance with more complex tasks, like verifying their FAFSA or reviewing their financial aid award letter. In sum, we constructed ten message templates to convey all of the key information students would need over the summer. Examples of two of these message templates follow. The fields in bold were customized to the student and/or the college he or she planned to attend.

Message purpose: Remind students to register for orientation

Hi **Sylvia**! Have you signed up for the **MSU** orientation? Last one is **7/15**. Need to register? **www.tinyurl.com/msuorient**. Need help? Reply MTG to talk w/ an advisor.

Message purpose: Offer to help with financial aid application or award letter

Hi **Sylvia**! Need help w/ the FAFSA? Questions about your fin. aid award letter, or need more aid? Reply MTG to meet with a **DISD** counselor.

With 1,600 characters of information across the ten messages and the offer of one-on-one professional assistance, we hoped to make a meaningful dent in summer melt among our partner districts.

Logistics and Fine Tuning

In addition to identifying a system for message delivery, a text messaging campaign requires attention to several details. While the sites had signed on, in principle, to the text intervention, we still had to finalize the high school exit surveys that each district would administer to collect student contact and college intention information; facilitate data sharing agreements between each partner and Signal Vine to allow for the transfer of this student-level information; and train the counselors who would respond to students' requests for help over the summer.

The exit survey took a different form in each site. Because uAspire had financial aid advisors in each of the high schools participating in the intervention, the advisors gathered much of the contact and college intention information directly from students, one by one. Dallas ISD had not previously used an exit survey and so created one to be administered across all of the high schools in the district. Each Denver high school already administered an exit survey and simply added a field for the student's cell phone number. Critically, in each site, legal counsel determined the districts had the authority to send text messages as part of their broader communication efforts with students and families, without obtaining prior consent.

Alex Chewning and Erin Cox at uAspire, Sylvia Lopez at Dallas ISD, and Cori Canty at Denver Public Schools were indispensable as site liaisons and provided invaluable insight into the design and structure of the intervention. Several key questions emerged from collaborative planning conversations. First, how would students react to receiving these college-related text messages seemingly out of the blue? Because the intervention was designed as a lottery where only some students would receive the messages, it was not possible to advertise the text messaging campaign in schools prior to graduation. Would students be suspicious about messages if they weren't expecting them or didn't know the sender? Chewning and Cox recommended the addition of an introductory message for each site that was ostensibly sent from someone the students either knew personally or at least knew by name, informing them that they would receive a set of college-related text messages over the course of the summer. uAspire sent the following introductory text to its students. The fields in bold were customized to each student:

> Hi **Alex**, this is **Brendan W.** from uAspire. We want to help you w/ college! Stay tuned for key summer To Dos. Save this #, you can txt us for help!

uAspire configured this introductory message to be associated with the financial aid advisor with whom each student had worked during the academic year. In Dallas and Denver, the introductory message came from the head of school counseling and the superintendent, respectively. The level of personalization in the introduction appeared to have a strong influence on how students responded to the text messages; uAspire students were more likely to respond with enthusiasm, excited to hear from the advisor with whom they had worked closely during the school year.

Lopez posed another important question related to families: Could we also message parents? There were several compelling reasons to send a similar set of messages to parents. Parents exert a strong influence on students' educational decisions. If they could be better informed about the summer college-related tasks their child had to complete and could easily ask questions of a counselor, perhaps they would be better able to support their child's college aspirations. Chewning, Cox, and Canty agreed about the value of messaging parents wherever possible, and each site modified its data-gathering procedures to collect parent contact information as well. In the Dallas schools, however, some parents had limited proficiency in English and would benefit from receiving the text communication in their native language. While we did not accommodate multiple languages, we did have the parent message templates translated into Spanish, given the high volume of Spanish-speaking families in Dallas. The introductory text message in Dallas allowed parents to opt to receive messages in Spanish.

Next, what should happen when students wrote back? As the message templates above illustrate, a core goal of the intervention was to make it easy for students to connect with a counselor by responding to one of the text messages. The reply "MTG" would automatically generate the help request e-mail to a student's designated counselor. But what would happen if a student wrote back something like, "I need help. Can someone call me?" At that time, the Signal Vine system was only configured to deliver the automated and personalized messages; it did not yet have the capacity to facilitate subsequent exchanges between students and counselors. However, the text campaign needed a system that could flexibly handle variation in students' replies.

To do this, Lin and Passarella created a message response portal, analogous in its simplicity and limited range of actions to an early 1980s Atari gaming console. The Signal Vine system would route students' or parents' anonymized responses to a web portal to which we would have access. Upon reading the message, one of three actions was possible: generate the help message to the counselor; cancel all subsequent messages if the student or parent asked that the messages stop; or automatically generate a text message with additional information about the intervention if the student or parent expressed skepticism about the credibility of the message.

TEXT CAMPAIGN LAUNCH

From among college-intending recent high school graduates in Dallas, as well as in the uAspire sites in Boston, Lawrence, and Springfield, we randomly selected a subset to receive the text message outreach, with the remaining students serving as a control group that received no intervention. Denver opted for a hybrid model through which students randomly selected for the intervention received counselor outreach supplemented with text messages.

Of college-intending students identified to receive the outreach, the actual share providing viable cell phone numbers ranged considerably across the sites, from 60 percent in Dallas to over 90 percent in the uAspire sites. This variation was not surprising. The Dallas district was administering its high school exit survey for the first time to a senior class of nearly eight thousand students. Survey administration practices differed across high schools, leading to higher response rates in some schools than in others. Students in Dallas may also have been less willing to provide cell numbers than those in the uAspire sites, where most students had strong personal relationships with individual advisors who were requesting students' contact information in person. Regardless, across the partner sites, thousands of college-intending students, many from low-income backgrounds, had provided cell phone numbers and would soon be receiving personalized reminders of the tasks they needed to complete in order to follow through on their college plans.

The first evening of the campaign, a Thursday in late June, arrived. Messages were slated to go out first in Dallas at 7 p.m. CST, given that this was a time when students and parents were more likely to be home and together. Shortly before this time, we logged on to the Signal Vine web portal, poised to respond to students' and parents' messages—but would any come in? We had no basis for estimating whether or the extent to which recipients would message back. In advance of the campaign's launch, educators to whom we described the project offered conflicting assessments. Many secondary and higher education officials expressed skepticism that students would want to receive college task reminders on their cell phones, let alone respond to these messages. After investing many months and thousands of dollars in designing a personalized messaging system, would students and their families engage?

Shortly after the first messages were sent, we experienced our own "Mark Zuckerberg moment." Responses started flooding into the portal at a much greater rate than we anticipated. With each refresh of the screen, fifteen to twenty new responses would come through. Some of these were grateful and detailed, students or parents asking for help with their college planning. Others were brief and noncommittal ("Thanks" or "OK"). Others expressed skepticism that the messages came from a source they could trust (e.g., "Who's this?"). Several parents indicated a preference to receive the messages in Spanish. Few recipients, however, asked that the messages stop. An hour into the first night, we knew we were onto something. Text messages that had cost only pennies to send were catalyzing a steady volume of student and parent correspondence.

Response rates in the uAspire sites were particularly high, in large part because students thought they were responding to the personal cell phone of their school-year advisor (the ostensible sender of the introductory messages in these sites). Though some students expressed disappointment upon learning that that their responses were not going directly to their advisor, they nonetheless stayed engaged and often sought out support from uAspire. Response volume was greatest at the start of the campaign, particularly in response to messages offering help with financial aid, but it also accelerated later in the summer when messages offered students help interpreting their tuition bills.

Student and parent responses were generally positive, engaged, and focused on the key college-related issues that they were managing during the summer months. Financial aid was the most prevalent issue raised in response messages, with substantial focus on other topics such as student orientation, the health insurance waiver process, and placement test procedures. Broadly speaking, students and parents sent back four types of messages. First, respondents replied with general expressions of gratitude, particularly in response to the initial outreach:

> This is excellent news! I appreciate any support uaspire gives me and your assistance. Talk soon!

> Ok no problem . . . thanks for you guys still helping me out.

> Okay, thanks a lot for all the help so far as well, hope you enjoy the fireworks tomorrow ☺

> Everything u guys have done for me. I am grateful.

Second, parents and students wrote back to request help. One of the first messages was so in line with the kind of response we hoped to elicit that we could hardly have scripted it more perfectly: "Oh hey! You couldn't text me at a better time! I was wondering if I can make an appointment with you . . . I need to update my financial aid with the 2011 tax forms and I don't know how to do it. I need your help!" Other examples:

> I need to talk to my counselor.
>
> Please give me a call.
>
> Yes we do need your help i am not a texter as you can tell can you call me please.
>
> Yes she does need additional aid. Please help us.

Students and parents also messaged back to report on their plans and the progress they had made with specific preenrollment tasks mentioned in the text outreach. For example:

> He has already been to orientation.
>
> Yes i already paid deposit now need tb test.
>
> Hey my plans have actually changed. I'm going to bunker hill now.

A third group of respondents expressed a lack of interest in or need for the outreach. For example, "Thanks but i'm all set for the fall. I don't need anymore messages." But these responses were in the minority. Specifically, fewer than 4 percent of all recipients asked for the messages to stop over the course of the summer. Encouragingly, of those students who said they were all set and requested to stop receiving the messages, nearly all enrolled on time in the fall.

The balance of responses were short and hard to interpret (the "OK" and "Thanks" variety) or expressed skepticism, though when we provided additional detail about the intervention, students or their parents often wrote back with appreciation or to request assistance.

Among those for whom the sites had active cell phone numbers, response rates ranged from 50 to 60 percent across sites. These response rates were on par with the rates at which counselors had been able to make contact with students through direct outreach efforts the previous summer (as described in chapter 4). The resounding difference was that here, students and parents were communicating without the counselors having to devote any time or energy to outreach. Students and parents were reporting on how they were doing and raising their hands, virtually speaking, to ask for help. The uAspire advisors who had been involved with both models—reaching out to students directly versus utilizing the automated text platform—were solidly in favor of the text-based approach.

Depending on the site, one in five to one in three students who provided a working cell phone number requested help from a counselor, though a lower share of students actually met with a counselor. This may have been due in part to the portal limitations, which prevented counselors from responding rapidly and personally to students' messages, and in part to counselor practices. In some cases, days passed between the time counselors received help request e-mails and when they followed up. Indeed, some messages from students and parents revealed that they were not necessarily getting the help that they were expecting: "Hey, I called the other number you gave me but you didn't answer." Particularly when reaching out via text, students and parents may expect more rapid response from someone on the other end, and may be less likely to take up a counselor's offer to meet when there is a lag between the request for assistance and the counselor's follow-up.

Data from the National Student Clearinghouse provided evidence that an intervention as simple and low-touch as personalized text reminders of required matriculation tasks can generate substantial increases in on-time college enrollment.[7] We consistently found positive impacts of the text messages in sites and among subgroups that lacked access to quality college-going support and information, either during the school year or in the summer after high school graduation. For instance, in Lawrence and Springfield, where there are few school- or community-based college counseling resources upon which students can draw, the text messages increased enrollment by over 10 percent, from an enrollment rate

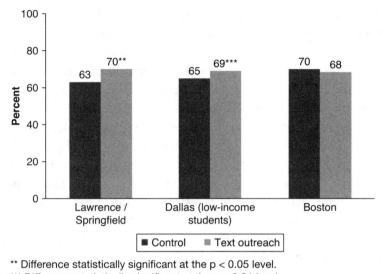

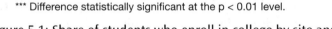

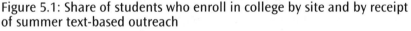

** Difference statistically significant at the p < 0.05 level.
*** Difference statistically significant at the p < 0.01 level.

Figure 5.1: Share of students who enroll in college by site and by receipt of summer text-based outreach

of 63 percent for students who did not receive outreach to 70 percent for those who did (figure 5.1). We observed similar substantial increases in enrollment in Dallas among low-income students (e.g., those who qualified for free- or reduced-price school meals), who were less likely to have benefited from family guidance through the college process or from school-based supports, given the limited time that school counselors have to spend on college preparation. Both groups of students stood to benefit considerably from the information and prompts provided by the text messages.

On top of these positive impacts, the text message campaign cost only $7 per student, inclusive of hiring counselors to provide help when students requested assistance. This type of intervention could be scaled at low cost to reduce summer melt and increase college going, particularly among would-be first-generation college students. Even more broadly, this approach could be applied both earlier in the college process, to positively influence completion of college-going steps as well as the types of colleges to which students apply, and after enrollment, to help students select courses and majors and to access academic supports once on campus.

It is worth noting that the text messaging campaign did not generate positive impacts in all sites. For instance, in Boston, which already has a high concentration of college-planning supports both during the school year and in the summer after high school, students who received the text messages were no more likely to enroll than students who did not receive the messages (see figure 5.1).

The positive results in some sites and for some students but not others begs the question of the mechanisms by which the messages may have impacted student decision making. On the one hand, response rates were quite high—approaching those observed in the more costly counselor outreach interventions. Yet the majority of recipients neither met with a counselor nor followed the task-specific web links (at least not from their mobile phones). If the intervention increased enrollment, it was likely for reasons other than connecting them to professional assistance or enabling them to complete tasks via their phones. Perhaps the messages simply prompted students to deal with tasks in the present rather than continually delaying them until the end of summer. Students with college-educated parents are accustomed to being prodded to keep up with education-related tasks. Perhaps these messages simply provided the information and nudge from which first-generation students could benefit but weren't receiving from other sources. This might explain why the messages had little impact in Boston, where students already had substantial access to high-quality college information and guidance. Or maybe the information in the text messages inspired students to reach out to their intended college rather than a counselor from their high school or a uAspire advisor.

Information gathered in the months following the summer campaign suggests that the text messages operated through many of these channels.[8] For example, the students surveyed said the messages were most effective at prompting them to complete tasks and at informing them of tasks about which they were unaware (table 5.1). Many respondents also felt that the text outreach

Table 5.1:   Follow-up survey of student responses to text message campaign

The text messages . . .	Percentage of respondents who felt that each statement was "somewhat true" or "very true"
Got me to complete a task I hadn't yet done	86%
Informed me about something I hadn't realized I needed to do	86%
Helped me manage my time better	75%
Got me to reach out to a uAspire advisor for help	72%
Helped make the summer tasks less overwhelming	70%

helped them manage their time, organize and plan tasks, and connect to an advisor if they needed additional help. These responses suggest that the messages leveraged several behavioral strategies to positively influence how students engaged in postsecondary planning and, as a result, their ability to successfully enroll in the fall following high school.

THE NEXT ROUND OF TEXTS

Like the counselor outreach model, text messaging has been utilized in locations across the country. One organization that has worked to integrate text messaging into its practice is iMentor in New York City. iMentor pairs low-income students with volunteer adult mentors in the community who forge long-term relationships with their mentees. The mentors help students navigate the college process and develop skills that position them for college success. One challenge iMentor has encountered in the past is how to provide mentors and mentees with all the information the mentees need to successfully matriculate at one of the dozens of colleges and universities frequently attended by iMentor students.

During summer 2013, iMentor used personalized text messages to inform both mentors and mentees about tasks required for college matriculation. iMentor collaborated with community-based organizations and postsecondary partners in New York City to create enrollment tip sheets for the fifty-five institutions most frequently attended by students in the city; these tip sheets formed the basis for the text messages that iMentor sent out. The messages were similar to those in our text intervention but also reminded students of additional procedural tasks, like submitting immunization records and final transcripts. In the iMentor text campaign, both students and mentors were able to opt in or out of the messages; approximately 90 percent of each group elected to receive the messages.

Though iMentor has yet to observe impacts of the text campaign on students' college enrollment, overall response rates and survey feedback were very similar to what we found in our text campaign. Approximately 25 percent of all recipients responded at some point during the summer, with 20 percent of recipients requesting help from an iMentor program coordinator. The text campaign had a strong impact on the mentors, 97 percent of whom reported that the texts were useful. As with Karen Arnold's survey findings in the uAspire sites, iMentor recipients reported that the messages were most effective at prompting them to complete a task in a timely fashion and informing them of tasks about which they were unaware.

The Minnesota Office of Higher Education (OHE) also piloted a program in two Twin Cities high schools through which they sent graduates personalized reminders of important college-related tasks to complete during the summer. OHE staff traveled to each school to describe the project and invite students to sign up for the messaging campaign. OHE offered students the option of choosing outreach by text, e-mail, or Twitter. Interestingly, the selected method of outreach differed considerably across schools, with most of the students in one school selecting text while most of the students in the other school chose e-mail. Virtually no student opted to receive messages via Twitter.

Another difference from the other text message campaigns was that student responses to the personalized reminders were fielded by an OHE staff member rather than by a counselor or mentor connected to the educational organization working directly with the student. While the OHE staff member did not have formal training in the college or financial aid process, she knew enough based on working with the statewide aid programs to answer most questions. Equally important, in the staff member's opinion, was her ability to encourage students to persist in their communication with their intended college to obtain answers to their questions about financial aid or matriculation requirements.

The responses that Minnesota OHE received mirrored the feedback from the other text campaigns. More than half the recipients in the school where most students opted for text outreach responded at least once, with students expressing gratitude for the reminders and revealing that they had completed important tasks like attending orientation or registering for courses. The text reminders also provided students with an effective channel for raising questions or describing challenges. For instance, one student replied, "I have gone to orientation and made my class schedule but I have not yet set up a payment plan. I'm really stuck at what to do next. Help?" Also indicative of the potential efficacy of text messaging were the responses from the school where most students signed up for e-mail outreach. Students there were less responsive overall, and when they did respond, it was typically well after the initial message had been sent. Students reported that they didn't check their e-mail often, and in some cases, had missed completing tasks because they had not seen the reminder soon enough. Based on the success of the pilot, Minnesota OHE is repeating and scaling up the project to serve more students in subsequent summers.

Another organization working to implement a text messaging strategy is the West Virginia Higher Education Policy Commission. In rural settings like West Virginia, students often live dozens of miles from their school. This geographic spread poses challenges in situating college planning resources that many students can access. This, among other factors, may contribute to West Virginia having one of the lowest college-going rates of any state in the country. The fact that it is challenging to provide in-person support to students who are so geographically dispersed makes personalized text messaging all the more attractive as a way to deliver high-quality college information.

To capitalize on the potential of text messaging to increase college entry in the state, the commission facilitated a partnership between the fourteen West Virginia public high schools and the four higher education institutions most frequently attended by the high schools' graduates. Starting in winter 2014, high school seniors in participating high schools received messages about completing the FAFSA, reviewing financial aid letters, and choosing colleges. Messages continued into the summer to remind students about summer-specific tasks to complete and into the freshman year of college to notify students about academic and social supports available on campus. The West Virginia model is a strong example of the potential for educational agencies to leverage text messaging as an inexpensive technological solution to better facilitate students' successful transition from high school into college.

—◆—◆—◆—

CHAPTER 6

With a Little Help from My Friends
Peer Mentors Offer Summer Support

Yabielis (Yabi, for short) Guerrero was born and raised in the Bronx, the poorest of the five New York City boroughs. Yabi's mother emigrated to the United States from the Dominican Republic when she was pregnant with Yabi. She settled in the Bronx and has been there ever since. Yabi was a strong student throughout elementary school and high school. During middle school and high school, Yabi attended the Bronx School for Law, Government and Justice (LGJ), run by the Urban Assembly, a New York City–based network of schools founded in 1990 with the goal of supporting students from high-poverty communities through high school and into college. The Urban Assembly network includes twenty-four other schools, situated in four of the five New York City boroughs. "Since seventh grade, Yabi always took her education very seriously, was deeply committed to her school community, was humble and kind to others, and had a laser-sharp focus on getting to college," said Meisha Ross-Porter, Yabi's principal for six years at LGJ.

After graduating from LGJ, Yabi began her college education at Skidmore, a highly competitive liberal arts college in Saratoga Springs, New York. Skidmore is a prestigious and well-resourced institution. Yet it was not the college that Yabi had always dreamed of attending, not because she had her sights set on another college in particular, but because she "didn't know what a liberal arts college was, and had never heard of Skidmore." As Yabi explained, "It wasn't the kind of school I ever expected to see myself in because I didn't know such a place existed. I didn't know enough to dream of it." Nevertheless, she applied at the recommendation of her high school counselor, and after getting in, decided—with trepidation—to go.

Yabi did not face any summer barriers in getting to Skidmore. As part of the Higher Education Opportunity Program (HEOP) in New York State, she participated in a summer bridge program that brought her to campus at the end of June.[1] Ritu Sen, director of college readiness for the Urban Assembly, praised such programs as invaluable for students like Yabi. "Because students are supported with wrap-around transition services on the college side, our role on the high school side is just to ensure that they make it there at the start of the summer," she explained. "I wish every student in need had the benefit of college support like that."

In July following her high school graduation, Yabi moved to the Skidmore campus and engaged in an academically rigorous month of math, writing, and prefreshman seminar classes with mandatory tutoring. This prematriculation program was intended to prepare students for the academic rigor of freshman year. According to Yabi, the students "got honest feedback from professors on where [they] needed to improve academically." At the end of the month-long program, Yabi returned to the Bronx. The contrasts between Skidmore and her home community were striking. As Yabi said, "I had one foot in college and one still back home. I spent a 'weird' month at home and returned back to Skidmore in the fall to start college."

Despite getting an early taste of college through the summer bridge program, settling in during her freshman year was nonetheless challenging. "I'm from the Bronx," Yabi explained. "I had always lived around populations just like me. It was culture shock. It was challenging to adapt and see myself staying there for four years. When I got there, I didn't want to stay." And while helpful, the summer transition program didn't entirely prepare her for freshman year. "I found I was unprepared, and I had a hard time connecting to the environment."

Early into her first year at Skidmore, Yabi returned to her old high school to visit her counselor, Traceyann Guillaume, who had recommended Skidmore and with whom she developed a close relationship during her high school career. "Ms. Guillaume gave me pep talks," said Yabi. "She helped me to put things into perspective." With this support, Yabi persevered at college. Although she recognizes how different the environment is from her community in the Bronx, reflecting on Skidmore, Yabi now notes, "I am lucky to be here. I know that I'm one of the lucky few. I'm aware of my privilege. But I want more people here like me."

Yabi's desire to further diversify Skidmore, coupled with another recommendation from Gillaume, brought Yabi to serve as a college coach through the Urban Assembly's Bridge to College (BTC) program. Since the summer of 2006, the Urban Assembly has been deeply engaged in honing and expanding its BTC peer coach program, implemented in response to the issue of summer melt among its college-intending graduates. Richard Kahan, founder and CEO of the Urban Assembly, shared how the BTC program first emerged: "We discovered the problem of summer melt at the Urban Assembly anecdotally from principals when we first graduated a large number of students. Most educators assumed that if students graduated from high school and were admitted to college, they would show up sixty days later. It was hard to imagine, after seeing students on the proudest day of their lives at high school graduation, with financial aid arranged, and an acceptance to college in hand, not showing up in September. Every one of our principals could tell you their high school's graduation rate, but few had any idea whether their students showed up to college. When we first discovered this problem, and the dimensions of it (about half of Urban Assembly [college-accepted] students in 2006 were not showing up to college), we assumed there were models somewhere to target this type of problem. It turns out there weren't, so we invented ours."

The college coaches who staff the Bridge to College program are former Urban Assembly graduates who are currently enrolled and succeeding in college. They serve as summer peer mentors for all college-intending graduates from their assigned high school, typically the school from which they graduated only a year or two earlier. The coaches are armed with background information on the graduates from each school's counselor (many of whom are on vacation in the summer) and are under the close supervision of central Urban Assembly leadership and three expert Urban Assembly school counselors dedicated to supporting the program over the summer. With this support, peer coaches are responsible for reaching out to recent graduates from their assigned school and supporting them as they complete all of their prematriculation tasks and generally get ready for college in the fall. The peer coaches adhere to a well-articulated structure that Bridge to College leadership has developed for supporting students with summer tasks. Yet they maintain sufficient flexibility that coaches are also able to assist with the unscripted life challenges that their assigned students face.

By the summer of 2013, the Bridge to College program worked annually with approximately a thousand students from the fourteen Urban Assembly high schools in New York City, with each coach managing a caseload of seventy-five to a hundred students. In recent years, the Urban Assembly has also collaborated with the City University of New York's At Home in College Initiative and College Access: Research and Action (CARA) to replicate and deepen its model to serve even more students throughout New York City.

Invigorated by serving as a Bridge to College coach during the summer after her freshman year, Yabi returned to Skidmore for her sophomore year and in that time, really came to love the college. For Yabi, working as a BTC coach provided "inspiration not to quit." As Yabi reflects, "There I was, serving as a role model to other people. What would it look like for me to transfer back to the city? Coaching other kids through the summer made me see how important it was to stay at Skidmore, complete my four years, and not give up on myself. I returned, became more involved in activities, and felt more encouraged to succeed myself."

THE POTENTIAL POWER OF PEERS

For many reasons, near-aged peer-based support is a promising approach to support positive youth outcomes, particularly for recent high school graduates. One advantage that near-aged peers bring is their greater ability to reach and connect with students, in large part because of their facility with the modes of communication students most frequently use, but also because recent high school graduates often relate more easily to near-aged peers. As Yabi describes it, "I'm able to relate in a way that counselors can't. Counselors will see students in school and then call their house. I would find their cell phones and text them. I would Facebook-stalk them—find their friends on Facebook to get to them. It's trying different tactics. Try Facebook, try texting, try calling. I was hunting students down. I would be calling them day and night. Whatever a student needed. Accommodate. This is key."

Peer coaches may also be able to overcome relational or other institutional barriers that stand in the way of counselors connecting with students over the summer months. Some students may be hesitant to engage with an adult, even an excellent counselor with whom they have had a close relationship. "Even if the counselor begged the student to come in, some students weren't really responsive," explained a Bridge to College coach. "We had a closer bond. It was like, 'You're closer in age. I'll listen to you. You did this last year.'" This applied to the offer of general support as well as outreach related to specific college-related tasks. "Like with award letters and tax transcripts, when I posted on Facebook and explained that you had to do this in order to get to college, that's when everyone turned around and ended up doing it." Another coach agreed: "When you deal with someone your own age versus an adult, you say more of what you need. The student can connect with you. Their counselor did all of this [college-transition processes] so long ago. [Coaches] can tell [the students] about recent experiences."

As these reflections suggest, students sometimes feel more comfortable seeking and receiving advice from peer mentors. The same can sometimes be said about talking to parents, as Yoscar Ogando's experience as a coach illustrates. A couple weeks after high school graduation, Yoscar's phone rang. "Yoscar, I'm freaking out," Danny declared. "I got my financial aid package, but I don't really understand it." Danny was sheepish about discussing the issue of paying for college further with his family, as he recognized the stress that the topic of college financing was placing on his parents. Instead, Danny confided in Yoscar that there was a $5,000 gap between his aid package and the cost of attending his institution. Danny had no idea how he would pay this. When Yoscar sat with Danny to review his financial aid award letter, the first thing Yoscar noticed was that Danny's aid package did not include TAP (or Tuition Assistance Program) funds. TAP is a need-based grant program in the state of New York through which eligible, full-time college students can receive up to $5,000 in grant aid to help cover the costs associated with attending college in New York. "I was told that I wasn't eligible," Danny said, when Yoscar asked about it.

It didn't make sense to Yoscar that Danny wouldn't be eligible for TAP. Together, they returned to Danny's online TAP application. At first everything looked okay. As they continued through the application, however, they noticed that Danny had accidentally reported his father's income as if it were his own. This simple mistake was enough to render Danny ineligible based on the program's criteria—Danny appeared too wealthy to qualify. To rectify the problem, Danny and Yoscar had to find proof that Danny did not actually make that much income himself. After a week "or three," as Yoscar noted, they were able to get the issue settled and Danny was able to receive TAP funds for the first year of college. If it hadn't been for Yoscar's support, he might have failed to enroll or done so with unnecessary financial burden.

Yoscar was able to devote considerable time to working side by side with Danny to identify and rectify the error in his TAP application. As the Bridge to College coaches and the Urban Assembly counselors have all recognized, it would likely have been challenging for a school counselor to devote this level of time and personal attention. Another coach emphasized, in addition to the ease of communication between peers, the flexibility that she offered in being available at times when the student would want to engage. "I'm a friend who you can call at twelve o'clock to get help—advice, friendship, and help all together. We are all students. The attraction and communication is easier [as well as] the ability to speak and be open. I can use my way to respond—'oh, I feel you'—this is something that they won't have from a counselor."

Working with a peer mentor may also help to shift students' perceptions about who goes to and succeeds in college. First-generation college goers are often uncertain about whether they belong in college; they may also question whether students "like them" feel comfortable and/or are successful on campus. Prior evidence demonstrates that peer mentor outreach can have a positive impact on high school seniors' engagement in the college process.[2] Students' views about their own potential for collegiate success might be reinforced by talking with someone their age who grew up in the same community, attended a similar (or even the same) high school, and was now enrolled and thriving in college. As one

BTC coach explained, "The students want to talk to someone closer to their own age who went through all of this already."

Another coach described her assigned students' reactions to her offer of support: "I went to this school and the students knew me. They could say, 'She's cool. I know who she is.'" These peer coaches could share firsthand how they dealt with and overcame challenges similar to what the student was experiencing. They could also describe how they successfully managed the summer transition. "We can offer our perspective," explained one coach. "Not too long ago, I did the same process. Even though I made some mistakes, I let my students know that it's not going to be picture perfect. You are going to face some challenges when you go, when you register. Counselors aren't so old that they can't remember, but the whole process is different from when they went to college. We are up to date."

Working with a peer mentor can also help students gain a more concrete understanding of college life and what situations they may experience on campus. Bridge to College coaches reflected on their willingness to give students a realistic understanding of what college is really like and what challenges students can expect to face once there. "We are able to be realistic," explained a coach. "You have to be honest with them. Keep it straight." Another coach added, "We talk about work and fun stuff, but tell them they have to balance the fun."

Finally, peer coaches are able to bring energy to summer college-going support. Ritu Sen describes the motivation the coaches bring to their work as needed "muscle." The Urban Assembly counselors do not work during the summer. Rather, they are ten-month New York City Department of Education employees. Even though they are not working in the summer, many make themselves available to provide feedback and guidance to the coaches on particular students. As Sen describes, the school-year counselors provide "3-1-1 backup, when needed."

The coaches are able to contribute to students' college planning even before the summer. Though school counselors support graduating seniors as far along in the matriculation steps as possible, during the spring they are also responsible for preparing the rising seniors for the college application process. As Rachel Beck, college counselor at the Urban Assembly School for Law and Justice explains, "It is incredibly hard to give all of the students that we serve the attention that they need in order to navigate the process that follows getting accepted to college. Having a BTC coach is invaluable to a counselor. All of my coaches have been first-generation college students. They understand what it takes to get through this process if there is no one at home to help out. My coaches . . . were able to help some of the more fragile and hard-to-reach students because I could not leave the building or spend an afternoon helping one student when I had hundreds of students depending on me." The BTC coaches are able to augment and reinforce the counselors' matriculation work with graduates, serving "as muscle over the summer and a social-emotional safety net."

One coach describes this handoff concisely: "Counselors' job is to get them into college. My job is to make sure they do everything that they need to do in order to get to college." The peer coach model can work because the coaches "are so eager and have so much energy to help," Sen explains. "Even if the school-based counselors are working, they don't have the capacity to go to all of these kids and nudge them when they aren't in the school building. The peer mentors find students on Facebook, they reach out to their friends, and friends of friends, to offer support and let them know they're there. They accompany students on trips to the bursar's office, to orientation, to meet with friends who have attended the same college and can offer words of wisdom, even shopping to pick out sheets and towels. They are so resourceful in reaching the students in ways that we do not have the creativity to think up, nor the time to do."

The coaches themselves share this sentiment. "Counselors have a lot of students through the year," one coach explained. "In the summer, it's time for counselors to go on vacation. How I helped over the summer is, like, school ends and after that everything is on the student. I was able to text them, e-mail, call constantly. Some were annoyed! But I was able to remind them that it doesn't end with the acceptance to college." As another coach said, "I think that counselors do a good job with responsive students, but we have to make it up in the summer for the students who aren't responsive or aren't able to understand the way that she says it. Our job is to see through what the counselor can't do during the year." In these ways, the support that the coaches offer students, nudging and following up on college-related tasks, is much like the support and prodding that college-educated parents often provide.

BEING THERE FOR STUDENTS

Prior to high school graduation, the coaches work with their assigned high school's counselor to meet with students one-on-one to discuss the college transition. The coaches themselves identify this pregraduation start as critical and have advised that meeting even earlier would increase the success of the program. "It would be good to start with students [even] earlier. To start late in the game is beyond difficult, because they don't know who you are," explained one coach. Yabi was able to put this advice into action. "I introduced myself to the seniors during my winter break to reconnect and refamiliarize students with my face. When I came back in the spring, students knew who I was."

After the school year is over and the seniors have graduated, the coaches' primary task is to doggedly seek out, contact, and offer college transitional support to the students in their caseloads. Their initial outreach occurs through phone, text, and Facebook. When students are unresponsive to these efforts, the coaches demonstrate a singular determination and creativity about making contact. Sometimes they show up on the student's doorstep to catch them before they head out to work or to meet friends. In other instances the mentors and coaches enlist the students' friends or family to facilitate a connection. In these ways, the coaches embed themselves not just in their students' school but also in their community. As Sen puts it, being a coach is "like being a detective and figuring out how to access these students emotionally, physically, virtually, all of these ways, in order to be a safety net for the students."

Yabi recognized her need to mold and adapt her approach in order to reach each of the students with whom she worked. "I would make sure that I'm really nice, become their friend, make sure they tell me what is going on. Get them comfortable enough to talk to me. I need to be persistent and help students to see that I genuinely care. When I can't get them, I'll get their parents. I'll ask them personal questions. Maybe because of my age, I can become friends. I sit with them and learn their story before I work with them." In addition to showing genuine interest in her students, Yabi also recognized the importance of sharing her own background. "These are vulnerable students. I tell them my story as well. I need to show empathy, that I understand where they are coming from. They also need to understand me. Students often don't understand what they are being told. I was helping them to get to college, and they needed to understand that."

Once the peer coaches are able to establish a trusting relationship, they assist their assigned students in a number of ways. As Yoscar's experience with Danny reflects, the coaches are expert in understanding and supporting the steps that students need to accomplish to get to college in the fall. Coaches guide their assigned students to complete loan entrance counseling and sign their master promissory notes, take placement exams and correctly interpret their scores, obtain a physical and proof of all required immunizations, and provide proof of high school graduation to their intended college or university in addition to the many other required matriculation tasks detailed in previous chapters. But the work of the coaches sometimes goes far beyond the concrete steps related to the college transition. For instance, one coach shifted from trying to help a student with summer matriculation tasks to the more pressing need of identifying supports for her and her newborn baby. Others helped in managing complex family situations, such as a student who was immersed in helping his mother deal with a court case. The coaches and peer mentors maintained a steadfast commitment to and deep sense of responsibility for the students in their caseloads. As one coach put it plainly, "Hey, if you are messing up this step, you are messing up someone's life!"

Finally, as Yabi's experience with one student underscores, there is power in the coach simply being there for each student during the college transition, to serve as a support and guidepost, just as many middle-class and wealthier parents are for their children. At the start of the summer and through July, Jasmine had plans to attend a two-year college at one of the State University of New York (SUNY) campuses. By the end of July, however, she had changed her mind, instead opting to attend Medgar Evers College, one of the City University of New York (CUNY) campuses. Housing at her SUNY school of choice had not been finalized, and it became clear that Jasmine would not be in a position to follow through on her intended college plan. Because she was making this switch late, Jasmine had to go to the campus to take care of her registration and enrollment. Yabi accompanied Jasmine on these trips to campus. Each visit included waiting in long lines, seemingly unending spells in waiting rooms, and revolving trips from one building to the next for different forms. Yabi and Jasmine together had to return to the Medgar Evers campus more than three times before Jasmine was even able to register for courses. Sensing her frustration, Yabi knew that Jasmine was likely to give up on college altogether without her support and encouragement. As Yabi describes it, by the time that Jasmine was finally able to enroll and was set for the fall, "She was like, 'Thank you for coming. If you didn't wait with me, I wouldn't have waited.' Having [me] be there, physically present, helped her. I was traveling with students. This was helping them—the in-person, face-to-face contact. Physically sitting with them in the process . . . that really changed their choices and decisions."

Reflecting on her experiences, Yabi explains that being a successful coach is "all about being sincere and authentic. If you don't care about the students, they are going to see it, and they will reciprocate your effort." Working with eighty different students means you have to "work with eighty different personalities." For each, Yabi accommodated, persevered, shared her own personal experiences, and met "students where they were at." In all of these ways, the Bridge to College coaches made sure that they "gave [their students] all that [they] could."

TRAINING, TOOLS, AND SUPERVISION

The many advantages of peer outreach notwithstanding, employing college students to combat summer melt also requires additional investment in training, tools, and supervision to support their work. In fact, reflecting on the first several years of the Bridge to College program, Sen recognized that it did not initially have a well-articulated structure and scaffolding to support the coaches. As the program matured, however, the Urban Assembly leadership realized that they needed to develop a tight system to guide the coaches' work with students.

The coaches are only a few years out of high school. For most, working as a BTC coach represents their first professional job as well as their first experience providing structured advising to students and families. In recognition of the complex and challenging work that coaches undertake each summer, BTC now provides coaches with an intensive, three-day preservice training. Early on in the training, BTC staff members prompt the coaches to connect their own struggles in the months before college with the challenges their students are likely to encounter over the summer. Cassie Magesis, deputy director of college readiness for the Urban Assembly, kicks off training with a question to the coaches: "What is one thing that you found difficult during the summer before you started college?" The coaches eagerly dive into the conversation, and after a few minutes, Magesis follows up: "Everyone, no matter how committed and focused they are, faced barriers and potholes on the way to college. We all faced moments where it came into question whether or not we would successfully enroll in college. We know how hard it is. But you all made it. How did you guys do so? Because we understand how difficult it can be, and because we all know how important college is, and how great it can be, we are all fighting alongside our students to help them matriculate successfully to college—helping to achieve their dreams. You are helping them from your roles as coaches."

The BTC coaches are trained to focus on the concrete steps that students need to take in order to matriculate on time. "For a peer mentor model to work," explains Ritu Sen, "you need to make sure that the coaches are not in over their heads. You need high-level, content-specific training so that coaches feel equipped to handle issues. Some tasks are easy—having students complete the TAP form for New York State–specific financial aid and indicate on their application where they intend to enroll. Coaches become experts on this simple step because it is a significant barrier to matriculation with an easy fix. We empower the peer coaches to understand how to explain steps related to financial aid so that students aren't intimidated by them and can easily take proper action." Because such a large share of the Urban Assembly students who continue to college matriculate to a CUNY campus, the training emphasizes matriculation steps specific to the CUNY system, and partners with CUNY administrators to get real-time updates and helpful insider tips.

Despite this intentional focus on concrete matriculation tasks, the full list of summer milestones with which coaches are expected to help their students is substantial. The coaches are responsible for supporting and documenting the completion of their assigned students' many college-related tasks. Though the Bridge to College coaches had completed many or all of these tasks when they transitioned to college, many felt intimidated by the volume and complexity of helping their caseloads of students with these responsibilities. Yabi reflects on the BTC training: "It was intense. It was a lot of information in a short time. But, there were also a lot of people there to help us feel confident, a lot of support. If we felt overwhelmed and confused, they would help us. This helped us to feel better. But it also helped to see the perspective of the student. I was in a helping role, and I was still confused. I couldn't do this without the training. It breaks down the entire experience."

The Urban Assembly staff trains BTC coaches not only to inform students about the tasks they have to complete but also to follow up and confirm that each step has been accomplished. Magesis tells the BTC peer mentors during the training, "As coaches, it's imperative that we are familiar with the evidence that proves that each of these steps has been completed. I can't tell you how many times I've asked a student—okay, have you updated your FAFSA? To which the student replies, 'Ummm, maybe?' The only way I'll know for sure if that student has done that is if I can find proof that it's been completed. Simply put, it's not sufficient to take a student's word. Often times the student doesn't know, and the processes in which they must engage are confusing." For example, the Urban Assembly trains coaches not just to ask whether students have been flagged for FAFSA verification and if so, whether they have successfully verified their income and assets. Rather, the coaches are trained on how students can complete the verification process and know that it's complete by asking to review copies of Student Aid Reports and financial aid award letters.

The Urban Assembly leadership also invests substantial time and energy developing the coaches' organizational skills. Central to this is a coaching log that lays out for coaches and their students a road map of tasks they need to complete over the summer in order to successfully matriculate. Magesis refers to the log as the "structural backbone of each coach's work" and underscores the importance of the log to the coaches: "The log is everything in our process. We look at it often. You will spend all day on it." In concert with their work with students, coaches maintain up-to-date records in the log, documenting when students accomplish each summer task and the proof of task completion.

From the first day of training, the BTC staff ingrains in the coaches that they are responsible for impeccable upkeep of the log. This includes reporting weekly on interactions with and steps taken by each student in their caseload. In her work with students, Yabi recognizes the power of the logs not just for keeping her own work organized but for building credibility with her students. "I have a checklist and this helps me to show students what they need to do," Yabi explains. "They don't get offended that I'm bringing these things up because they're on my list." To motivate coaches to keep their logs well organized, the Urban Assembly rewards coaches whose logs are error-free at the end of summer. Nearly three-quarters of their coaches kept full and complete logs.

While the BTC training makes clear to the coaches that both the expectations and the stakes for their work are high, Sen and Magesis also emphasize that a robust system of support is in place for the coaches. In addition to the initial training, ongoing training and supervision for BTC coaches continue throughout the summer months. One of the key sources of assistance is a supervising counselor for each coach. As noted above, most of the Urban Assembly school counselors are off contract in the summer months. The Urban Assembly maintains three counselors on staff to serve as BTC supervisors. These counselors are geographically distributed in the Bronx, midtown Manhattan, and downtown Manhattan and supervise the coaches in their respective areas. Some of the interaction between coaches and supervisors occurs through the logs. Logs are stored on a shared Google drive, and this allows counselors to supervise coaches and monitor students' real-time progress toward matriculation benchmarks. The counselors also use the logs to communicate about possible red flags for the coaches and suggest additional supports from which the student might benefit.

Another key mechanism for support is weekly or twice-weekly meetings with supervising counselors. Not only do these meetings provide a venue to ensure that students are receiving high-quality support, they also offer the counselors and coaches an opportunity to develop deeper relationships and maintain motivation and inspiration for the summer work. As Sen describes, "The supervisor is meant to help troubleshoot when the coaches are stuck. The supervisors are also content experts when the coaches need help with things like FAFSA, CUNY, and other issues. For example, one student needed to call LaGuardia Community College and had been placed on hold but doesn't have a lot of battery in his phone. How can this student get the call done in ten minutes? The supervisor can help the coach to find a direct number." Given that many of the coaches expressed an interest in working as college counselors one day, these meetings also provided them with a chance to learn firsthand how counselors and advisors approach working with students.

The Urban Assembly staff also organize four group meetings of all the coaches during the summer. The coaches are scattered throughout the city, working in the school and surrounding neighborhood to which they are assigned. The group meetings, according to Sen, are "equal parts group therapy and professional development." Bringing all of the coaches together provides an opportunity to troubleshoot common problems that arise, review exemplary log entries, network and collaborate, and take care of administrative matters, such as paying the coaches. Distributing paychecks during these sessions introduces a level of accountability, ensuring that the coaches are present and participate in each of the four summer meetings.

Coaches reflected that both the weekly meetings with their supervisors and the larger full-group coach meetings with the Urban Assembly leadership were essential, for different reasons. The full-group meetings "helped me out with the logs," one coach explained. "The smaller meetings [with supervising counselors] are to talk about the emotional side of the job. Both pieces are needed for ongoing support and training."

Hand-in-hand with a well-articulated system of supervision is the recognition that there are limits to the situations that peer coaches should be expected to handle independently. Supporting students through the summer months often means that coaches encounter weighty personal and financial issues with which students and families grapple during the college transition period. The coaches themselves recognize their limits in handling these issues. One BTC coach describes a typical example: "At-home situations, [where parents are] discouraging the student from moving on to college. I think that if it's out of hand at home, the counselor can go and settle that. We are still viewed as students. We are young. You can try your best. You can speak professionally in a nice tone, but sometimes they won't see you as an adult." Another coach agreed: "Parents are very difficult. They scare me. They say, 'You look young. How old are you?'" Recognizing this reality, the BTC structure allows the coaches to call on their supervising counselor to provide support and to step in, when needed.

IMPACTS AND OUTCOMES

Since the inception of Bridge to College, the Urban Assembly has focused most on honing the program design and delivery, and is beginning to more rigorously assess the impact of the Bridge to College program on its students' college-enrollment outcomes. The Urban Assembly was early to track its college enrollment numbers through the National Student Clearinghouse, numbers the New York City Department of Education now uses to hold its high school principals accountable for their students' post-secondary success. It is worth noting that from 2006, when the program began, through 2009, on-time college enrollment among Urban Assembly graduates rose from 48 percent to 75 percent. In fact, the enrollment rate of 75 percent has held steady for the three most recent years of the program—"about the time," in Sen's words, "[the Urban Assembly] figured out how to run the program really well."

Beyond this impressive trend, the BTC experience generated many ancillary benefits for the coaches. The peer-led outreach model fosters a tremendous sense of empowerment, both for the students receiving the outreach and for the coaches themselves. Moreover, the coaches discover that the training and experience they gained through their summer experiences pays dividends to their own college career. As one coach described the experience, "I liked this job. It helped me with my school stuff. I know what to hand in. . . . My mom is shocked that I know all of this and I'm on top of everything."

While the coach position is intended to be part-time—twenty hours per week—they go "all out," many working forty to fifty hours per week. They are motivated and eager to dig into the work. According to Sen, "The coaches understand how instrumental they can be. They get a real sense of satisfaction tied to work that a lot of them haven't had up until that point. It's a job that motivates them to do extra work. When every person on the team is working extra hours, you know that there is something going on with the magical quality of the group." Sen continued, "By the end of the summer, coaches recognize the value of loving a job, and are grateful for the experience. Everyone is empowered by the work that they are doing. They are doing work that adults aren't necessarily able to do. The coaches each have a story where they were able to reach a student that the adults in the school were not able to reach."

One coach reflected on the experience in this way: "There are few opportunities where college students get to impact people's lives at all. This job helped me to see that you can actually do that as a college student. I get these calls like, 'Thank you for getting my daughter into college.' I talked with my friends about their summer jobs and they say, 'Oh, I did office work, I shredded paper all day,' and I say, 'Oh, well I helped this student go to college.' It's just an amazing thing to say and it makes me feel good. I just put my all into this job and it showed results. It's really positive."

Sen further explained that the peer coach model creates an opportunity for deep professional exploration. "Many of the coaches are low-income and career-focused in their college work. Some of the coaches have been interested in helping professions and social services. They want to become educators, school leaders, social workers, counselors. One of the cool things has been to bring them into the community to learn about adults who support schools in all sorts of different ways. This gives the coaches some new ideas about what a job looks like day to day." By the end of the summer, many of the coaches report wanting to become college counselors. According to one coach, "This job has helped me to understand how important it is for people to be supporting these kids, but I think that they need a stronger foundation. They don't have a sense of self-accountability and responsibility. I don't think that this program can help that. They need to get that from elsewhere, but this program helped me to understand that this is really important. I'm interested in continuing in the education field."

The peer-based approach also allows the coaches to develop their own professional and advocacy skills. According to Sen, many of the coaches become resident experts and help their friends in college. "So true," Yabi corroborated. "I've helped friends and other family members with all of this. You are learning yourself and helping others." When they go back to campus, they help their friends with their college-related paperwork; they remind their friends about important tasks like FAFSA renewal. As one coach said, "This is giving me a concept of the whole matriculation process. Like, I was talking to my friend who just graduated. He was [planning on] going to college and I was asking him a few questions. My friend didn't verify his residency and I gave him information on how to do it. I felt like a great help. I was like, 'Wow, I can do this on my own. Where's my salary at?!' So I felt good about that—helping people that were not in my caseload." Another coach explained that her work as a coach helped her to understand things that she and her friends needed to handle differently, "I had problems with my financial aid last year and again this year, but now I know how to handle it by myself. I also helped my best friend. She transferred, and I was able to help her out. As another coach put it, "You learn tricks to get more money from the school. I don't think you're supposed to say that, but it's true!"

Even more broadly, the coaches experience firsthand the power of seeking help. Yabi reflected, "I think that one thing that I've learned is that I don't always have the answers, but that there is help. I have to admit it. It's about learning to ask for help, communicating in order to get it." And finally, the coaching experience instills in the coaches the hope that they are changing the trajectories for the students they serve. "Working with Bridge to College is motivating for me," added Yabi. "I want more people like me here [at Skidmore]. Hopefully in ten years, there will be way more students from inner-city areas in colleges like this."

A PEER APPROACH TO SUMMER COLLEGE CONNECT

In the summer of 2012, uAspire stepped into the arena of peer-based summer support for the first time. By that summer, uAspire had extended its reach beyond the Boston Public Schools. In partnership with its sites in Boston, Lawrence, and Springfield, Massachusetts, as well as with the Mastery Charter Schools in Philadelphia, Pennsylvania, uAspire designed and implemented an intervention to test the efficacy of peer mentor outreach as a strategy to reduce summer melt. The peer mentor program was implemented in parallel with the text messaging campaign described in chapter 5.[3] As with the counseling and text-based interventions discussed in the previous two chapters, we collaborated with uAspire and Mastery to conduct randomized controlled trials to evaluate the impact of the peer mentor outreach model on students' college outcomes.

Much of the peer mentor program design was informed by the insights from BTC, which by then was well established as a comprehensive and well-structured program. Both the uAspire and Mastery sites matched peer mentors with supervising advisors. Across sites, twenty peer mentors were hired to work with nearly a thousand college-intending high school graduates. The peer mentors were all graduates from the same public school system, and in some cases the same school, as the students with whom they would be working. They were mainly juniors and seniors in college, with most attending four-year institutions. In the Mastery site, the peer mentors followed the BTC model of serving a caseload of students from a single campus and receiving supervision from a counselor within their assigned site. The uAspire peer mentors worked out of the central offices in Boston, Springfield, and Lawrence and were supervised by teams of uAspire advisors. Diverging from the BTC model, the uAspire and Mastery peer mentors did not begin working with students until after the close of the academic year.

The uAspire and Mastery peer mentors worked side by side with their supervising advisors in central school or office locations, in contrast to the BTC coaches, who worked within both the schools and communities where they were assigned. uAspire and Mastery leadership were particularly emphatic on drawing a bright line to demarcate the type of assistance that peer mentors would and would not offer to their students. Specifically, mentors did not work on tasks that would require students to share financial information for themselves and/or their families. While the uAspire and Mastery peer mentors might help students review an award letter, for instance, they would hand over the task of helping students verify the FAFSA to a supervising advisor, since this might require access to family financial records. This guiding principle was important to both uAspire and Mastery, both of which wanted to protect students' privacy and avoid putting mentors in the position of helping students through complicated financial tasks that were beyond their training or experience. Because the uAspire and Mastery peer mentors had smaller caseloads, it was more feasible to pass along challenging circumstances that required further expertise and attention.

Similar to the experience of the BTC coaches, the uAspire and Mastery peer mentors felt fulfilled by serving in a peer-advisory role. As one of the uAspire-based mentors reflected, "I enjoyed working this summer, and I learned so many things . . . I enjoyed reaching out to the students, and I hope I made an impact on them for their future. They definitely made an impact on me just by trusting me and accepting my help on their transition to college. I felt so proud when I saw their smile and when they thanked me for helping them in their college issues." The peer mentors also recognized the ways in which they developed through serving as a peer mentor. Another mentor described the benefits this way: "This internship was a great experience to learn public speaking skills, group leader skills, peer mentor skills, and teamwork, and this will benefit me for my future in college and career. I recommend that uAspire continue this internship to help not only high school students get ready for college but to help college students gain knowledge and so they can have this great experience."

Students who received peer mentor outreach were substantially more likely to enroll on-time in four-year institutions. Peer support was particularly helpful for students who intended to enroll in college as of high school graduation but hadn't yet chosen a school. For these students, peer-based outreach increased timely enrollment by nearly nine percentage points (see figure 6.1).

Because they were not as far along in their college planning, these students in particular may have benefited from the additional

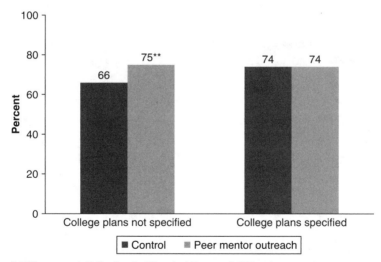

** Difference statistically significant at the p < 0.05 level.

Figure 6.1: Share of students who enroll in college according to the specificity of their college plans and receipt of summer peer-based outreach

guidance and support that the peer mentors provided. Though not as inexpensive as the text-based outreach, the peer-based approach, at approximately $90 per student, was nonetheless quite cost effective. Therefore, for educational agencies that want to provide summer support but lack the technical capacity to run a text-based approach and/or the financial resources to hire professional school counselors to conduct outreach, a robust peer-led model offers an affordable strategy—one that has the potential to improve college success not only for the college-intending students served but also for the peer coaches, who are indelibly shaped by the mentoring experience.

PART III

Implications for Practice and Policy

CHAPTER 7

◆ ◆ ◆

Assessing and Addressing Summer Melt
What High Schools and
Community Groups Can Do

As we have shared our work on summer melt with a variety of audiences, including policy makers, researchers, and educators, we have been continually struck that almost everyone has a story, either about themselves or about a person they know, related to the challenges students encounter during the summer after high school. One colleague, himself a first-generation college student, told how he unwittingly paid out-of-state tuition to attend a public college in his home state. Because he never corrected this mistake, he is still repaying his student loans to this day.

In this chapter we offer some practical guidance on what school districts, community-based organizations, and other education agencies can do to understand and take action on summer melt.[1] We address this chapter primarily to the secondary education sector, and specifically high school personnel. While colleges can and should investigate the extent of this problem among admitted students who make a tuition deposit, our experience has been that high schools and community-based organizations are most invested in examining melt rates among their high school graduates. Of course, the lessons here apply more broadly to organizations and individuals who seek to help students realize their college-going goals.

ASSESSING SUMMER MELT

Take a moment to think back to the students you met in chapters 2 and 3. Are there students whose stories strike a chord with you, or who remind you of students with whom you have recently worked? If your students are most like Adam (chapter 2)—from middle-class families with college-educated parents—then summer melt may not be a pressing problem. If, on the other hand, your students are from lower-income backgrounds or are the first in their family to go to college, then the summer may be an important area for investigation and investment to support students' successful transition to college.

Understanding the extent to which your college-intending graduates are struggling to realize their college plans is a critical first step in deciding whether a summer melt response strategy is needed in your educational setting. While the interventions profiled in the preceding three chapters are surprisingly inexpensive, educational budgets are nonetheless tight, and it's critical to ask whether a summer melt intervention would be a wise investment of resources to improve students' college outcomes. To assess the extent of summer melt among your college-aspiring students, you need accurate answers to the following two questions:

1. Which students intend to go to college in the fall immediately after high school graduation?
2. Of those who intend to go to college in the fall after high school graduation, which students successfully matriculate on time?

While the information that schools or education agencies need to assess the magnitude of summer melt is generally straightforward and relatively inexpensive to obtain, it is worth noting that linking records of students' college intentions to their actual enrollment can be a nontrivial process. Therefore, it may help to enlist the assistance of individuals with expertise in data management. In some districts, such persons can be found among your own district staff. In other districts, you may need the help of outside partners. Having identified the appropriate partners, you should be ready to dig into these two key questions to investigate summer melt.

Which Students Intend to Go to College in the Fall Immediately After High School Graduation?

Implementing an exit survey near the time of high school graduation is an excellent option to gather information on seniors' college intentions. This survey need not be complicated (see appendix B for a survey used by the Dallas Independent School District). The core information to collect is whether your students have applied and been accepted to college, whether they plan to go to college in the fall, and if so, where. The availability of simple, web-based survey technology—often integrated into student data management software like Naviance—means that schools can typically administer an exit survey and identify the college-intending students among the graduating class within several weeks.

There are several additional steps you can take to enhance the value of data collected through a high school exit survey. First, administer the survey as close to the end of the school year as possible. This will increase the chance that students have completed important steps in the college choice process and have a clear sense of where they plan to enroll. Second, to maximize survey response rates and therefore get a comprehensive picture of summer melt, make the survey a graduation requirement or offer an incentive, such as a prize raffle, for completing the survey. Third, ask students about their college plans both generally, by asking, "Do you plan to go to college in the fall?" and specifically, by asking, "Where do you plan to enroll?" If a student answers yes to the first question but is unable to answer the second, this may indicate that the student needs college-going support. For example, this pattern might emerge among students who intend to enroll in a local community college but who have not yet completed their application, given rolling admissions processes. These students in particular may stand to benefit from summer support.

For each student who indicates a specific college, further ask whether the student has paid a deposit (or sought a deposit fee waiver) and has received a financial aid package. If a student answers no to either of these questions, this may be an early indication that the student is already behind on some college-related tasks. For example, many students incorrectly think that their financial aid applications are complete even if they have not received a financial aid award letter. They may assume the college will just automatically factor financial aid into the tuition bill. Finally, the exit survey provides a valuable opportunity to collect updated student contact information, including cell phone numbers, e-mail addresses, and Facebook usernames. Having up-to-date contact information greatly improves the chance of successfully reaching students during the summer, if you plan to implement a summer melt response strategy.

Of Those Who Intend to Go to College in the Fall After High School Graduation, Which Students Successfully Matriculate on Time?

Currently, the best source of information on individual students' college-going outcomes is the National Student Clearinghouse (NSC). High schools, colleges, and other student-serving organizations can contract with the NSC to match college enrollment records with their student rosters and obtain data about students' college enrollment and persistence trajectories through the NSC's StudentTracker services. Records are matched by students' high school, name, and date of birth. The NSC records provide some additional information about students' college enrollment, such as whether each student is enrolled full-time or part-time, but do not indicate the specific courses in which students are enrolled. NSC data is typically provided on a semester-by-semester basis, making it possible to track students not only into but also through college. Of course, like any data source, the NSC is imperfect, but it remains the best source of information on whether and where students go to college.[2]

By connecting these two sources of data—information on each student's college intentions and actual enrollment data from the NSC records—you can identify the students who did and did not achieve their intended college plans, either because they selected a different postsecondary institution or because they failed to enroll entirely. A further step you can take is to add data about students' demographic characteristics and academic background. This makes it possible to analyze whether summer melt affects all students equally or is particularly prevalent among certain groups.

When you link up this data for the first time, like our partners at the Met, uAspire, Fulton County, and other school districts, you may be surprised to find that a large share of your college-intending students fail to attain their goal. The following section provides practical guidance on how to devise a response strategy that aligns with the level of resources that you can invest in the effort, the local context, and the student population you want to support through the summer months.

RESPONDING TO SUMMER MELT

As Erin Cox of uAspire has said to practitioners who are interested in responding to summer melt, "Don't worry about whether or not you are able to implement a program with all the 'bells and whistles.' If you find out that your students are struggling in the transition to college (and they likely are), just figure out what you can do and get out there and do something."

In identifying which approaches may work well for you, consider four factors: the quality of the information to which you have access about students' postsecondary plans; the resources you are able to devote to summer college-going support; the technology that you can leverage to increase the impact and reach of your efforts; and best practices for summer outreach that have worked in contexts similar to your own.

Information About Your Students' College Plans

One key to a successful summer melt intervention is being able to identify which of your graduating seniors plan to attend college in the fall. If you are not able to zero in on these students, you run the risk of devoting substantial time and resources to students with no intention of continuing to college. Therefore, as discussed above, we recommend collecting postsecondary intention information via a high school exit survey administered near the time of high school graduation. Armed with that data, you can focus on those students who have clear intentions for college or who have already accomplished several key steps, such as applying and getting accepted to college.

You may also want to consider ways that you can target those students who may be most at risk for summer melt. Summer melt tends to be more prevalent among college-intending students from lower-income backgrounds. If you serve a socioeconomically diverse population, you might consider targeting your efforts in schools serving the largest shares of students from low-income families. For instance, after finding that summer counseling had a pronounced impact on whether low-income students enrolled in college but no impact on enrollment outcomes of moderate-income and affluent students, Fulton County Schools in Georgia decided to focus future summer outreach efforts on the low-income students in the district. Before launching a summer intervention, do the investigative work to understand which of your students are most susceptible to summer melt and, therefore, which may stand to benefit the most from additional summer support. Don't be surprised, however, if strong patterns do not necessarily emerge. As one uAspire advisor reflected, summer outreach appeared to be beneficial for a great variety of students: "It was great to reach a huge diversity of students via Summer College Connect—from students who were going to top colleges and initially thought they were 'all set,' to students who still weren't admitted to community colleges. It confirmed to me that all of these students need our help over the summer."

Resources to Support Your Summer Intervention

In planning for a summer intervention, the next question to consider is what resources are available. A defining feature of all of the summer interventions we profiled is that students had the ability to access individualized and in-person assistance, from either a professional counselor or a peer mentor. Arguably, then, the most important resource you can make available is well-trained and caring adults who can help students navigate the summer transition to college. While we have typically relied on school-based counselors to conduct outreach efforts, summer interventions could also be staffed by other school personnel, by staff members from an area nonprofit or community-based organization, or by near-aged peers.

A first step is to identify potential employees who are eager and motivated to do this work. In the school districts and other organizations that have implemented summer outreach interventions, participating staff have been remarkably gratified by the experience. As a counselor from Fort Worth noted, much of her school-year work focused on students in crisis. In contrast, working with students over the summer to realize their college goals was a refreshingly positive experience. Other counselors stated that helping students over the summer was the type of work they had expected to engage in regularly when they decided to enter the counseling profession.

Similarly, after uAspire's first year of Summer College Connect, though the uAspire advisors acknowledged that the summer outreach undoubtedly increased their summer workload, they were nevertheless emphatic that the proactive summer advising had to become a standard part of their overall program model. As one advisor noted, "I really felt like I made a huge impact with the students who were able to come for appointments. Many of them came back a number of times because it took a lot of effort for them to work everything out." After this first summer, in fact, the uAspire advisors voted unanimously to continue with the program in subsequent summers.

Peer mentors have been equally invigorated and empowered by supporting students throughout the summer. An important question to think about is how to recruit peer mentors. One approach is to identify colleges or universities that large shares of your students have historically attended. It may be possible to work with staff at those schools to recruit students interested in returning to their community to serve as peer mentors over the summer. According to Ritu Sen of Urban Assembly and the Bridge to College (BTC) program, peer coaches need to have initiative and independence as well as "a bit of bravado [and] fearlessness, as a lot of [the tasks with which coaches engage] are so high stakes." Can you recall recent graduates who have these attributes and who might be interested in helping younger cohorts of students follow their path to college?

Having professional staff or peer mentors reach out to students requires a financial investment during the summer months. The counselor-led interventions in which we have been involved cost on the order of $150 per student, with each counselor receiving $4,000 to $5,000 in total compensation for summer work. Peer mentors typically cost less to employ. In the peer-based interventions, college students earned $2,000 for their work as summer mentors.

However, peer mentors require more management, oversight, and support than do professional counselors, both because they are young and because they need guidance to handle certain student circumstances, such as sensitive personal and financial situations. For instance, the BTC coaches expressed a preference that interactions with parents and families be handled by their supervising counselor. As one coach indicated, "Anything to do with the parents—the supervisor will be in on that meeting. While I try to lay the format for that respect, [parents still] see us as children.

Parents are thinking, 'What does this girl know. She is a child.'" Because making contact with students during the summer months takes persistence, peer mentors may also require more ongoing encouragement. Thus the additional management that peer mentors need typically means retaining professional staff who can support and supervise the peer mentor team.

Some of the districts and education agencies that have implemented summer counseling interventions have paid for them out of existing operating budgets; others have successfully applied for philanthropic funding to support summer outreach. Because the cost of staffing a summer intervention is often relatively low, several partners have been able to approach local or regional foundations for financial assistance. These funders typically have a much quicker turnaround than national foundations and are often interested in supporting work happening locally.

Related to program staff, it's also important to give careful consideration to the training they will need to best support students through the transition to college. School counselors who have provided summer college-going support felt that, though they were well equipped to help students with academic and social-emotional issues, they were less prepared to assist students with issues related to college matriculation, particularly financial aid. College students providing peer-to-peer support will be greener in all of these domains.

In preparing your own summer intervention, assess the skills and expertise of those who will directly support students during the summer. Based on this assessment, design and deliver training to equip your summer staff with the appropriate skills, information, and resources. Across interventions profiled in the previous chapters, issues related to financial aid were uniformly most common. Therefore, devote substantial training time to this topic—FAFSA filing, income verification, financial aid award review, financial aid appeals, loan entrance counseling, master promissory notes, and tuition payment plans, to name a few. If no one in your organization has expertise in these areas, investigate whether there is a state or local organization that can provide this training. For example, prior to the launch of Summer PACE in Fulton County, Georgia (chapter 4), program counselors received training on financial aid from the Georgia Student Finance Commission and a financial aid officer from Georgia Perimeter College. Also, organize information for your staff on the summer transition tasks required by the colleges and universities your students commonly plan to attend. Familiarize your staff with the specifics of these tasks as well as their associated deadlines, and provide them with information about whom to contact at each institution for further assistance.

Understandably, it may be daunting to consider training your staff to become experts in financial aid and college-transition processes. However, providing successful summer support doesn't mean staff members must become experts in all of the issues students may face; rather, they just need to be sufficiently familiar with the summer transition to help families navigate matriculation tasks and anticipate and address challenges that arise. As uAspire communicates to its advisors, "Students and families are expected to navigate [the summer] on their own, using paperwork and resources provided by the college. At the end of the day, a motivated professional trained in counseling will be able to dive into the paperwork, pick up the phone to the college, and otherwise advocate for students and families in a way that is quickly beneficial, even if she is not expert on all things going in." Alex Chewning of uAspire continues to explain, "Sometimes it's just about knowing how to *talk* to a financial aid office—what questions to ask, how to check for understanding, and how to advocate. In other words, if professional staff at least use the resources provided to students, they can inherently take advocacy to the next level."

Bringing Technology to Bear

Across the counselor-, advisor-, and peer-led interventions profiled in previous chapters, project staff devoted substantial time and effort simply to make contact with students. Incorporating automated and personalized outreach technologies into summer support programs can greatly increase staff efficiency and at the same time effectively communicate information about college-related tasks and deadlines directly to students. Because text messaging is the primary means by which high school and college students interact with each other, it is likely to be a more successful outreach technology than other communication strategies, such as e-mailing or automated ("robo") calling.

Implementing a text-based outreach strategy requires three critical pieces of information for each student: name, cell phone number, and where the student intends to go to college. This final piece of information makes it possible to personalize messages with institution-specific tasks that intending students are required to complete. Rather than attempting to send these messages directly, we recommend contracting with an organization specializing in text-based communication (such as our partner, Signal Vine) or examining whether this functionality can be built into your existing student data platform (as was done in the Austin Independent School District in Austin, Texas). Signal Vine and OneLogos Education Solutions (in Austin) were able to weave together the student contact data and college-specific task information, and thus populate text message templates for each required task with highly personalized information. The full set of these text message templates is available in appendix C.

One challenge to implementing a text messaging campaign is having accurate and active cell phone numbers for all targeted students. This can be a difficult goal to achieve. In certain sites where we have implemented text-based outreach, we were able to successfully send messages to only 60 percent of the students targeted. While texting is still less common among educational systems as a means of communication, it is growing in popularity. Therefore, school systems may want to identify other ways to collect cell phone numbers from both students and families—for example, during school registration or through annual efforts to update directory information.

If you have trouble collecting working cell phone numbers for some of your students, you may want to take a multipronged approach to outreach, sending personalized e-mails or postal letters to students for whom you did not obtain a cell phone number. Prior to graduation, you could also urge your college-intending students to join a college transition Facebook group. If your students typically matriculate to one of a small number of institutions, you could even consider creating college-specific groups. Establishing these groups prior to graduation provides a mechanism for messaging groups of students efficiently throughout the summer.

Finally, summer staff can make use of text messaging and other popular communication technologies even without automated outreach. The counselors and peer mentors profiled in earlier chapters used a variety of approaches, including e-mail and text messaging but also Facebook and phone calls. Sometimes they even tracked down students through their friends and parents.

Ultimately, personalized and automated messaging, supplemented with targeted personal outreach to students who are not responsive to the messaging campaign, is likely to generate positive outcomes for the most students during the summer months. Think of summer outreach like a political campaign. Political candidates work to connect with potential voters through a variety of channels—print media, television and radio commercials, web-based advertisements, and direct outreach. In your own campaign against summer melt, similarly try to employ multiple complementary strategies to provide important information to students and to connect them with professional assistance when they need help.

Implementation Best Practices

Across the intervention approaches profiled in the previous chapters, a number of program best practices emerge. One common thread is to start early. A key refrain from chapter 3 is that "summer melt starts in February." When asked how to improve upon the work of the BTC program (chapter 6), the coaches most often suggested that the program start earlier. High school counselors involved in providing summer outreach and support give similar feedback. Transition-to-college programs should therefore start soon after students have submitted their college applications. For many students, the timing should coincide with FAFSA filing (and, if required, the completion of income verification shortly thereafter). After students have received college acceptances, another key task is to help them review their financial aid award letters and assess which colleges offer them the right balance of affordability, quality, and academic fit. If you plan to provide outreach and support through the summer, publicize this to students well before graduation and create opportunities for students to get to know the counselors who will be available to help them over the summer. If possible, schedule initial counseling sessions with students before graduation. The various staff profiled here, whether counselors or peer mentors, devoted substantial time simply to making contact and setting up meetings with students, so scheduling meetings before the end of the school year could save your project staff precious time during the summer.

Second, be proactive. College-going support over the summer months will likely represent a sizable shift in standard practices, particularly within school districts. Therefore, set the expectation that counselors will be reaching out to students during the summer months. It is not sufficient for staff to just be available over the summer—proactive outreach is essential. Recall that in several of the interventions implemented by uAspire, all students were notified at the start of the summer that advisors were available for college-related support. Despite this clear messaging, very few of the students who did not receive outreach sought help from a uAspire advisor.

Third, establish credibility. If hearing from school-based staff over the summer is not typical for your graduates, building credibility in advance is critical. This is particularly true if you are using an outreach strategy like text messaging that you have not used with your students before. If students cannot clearly identify from the first message they receive who the sender is and why they should pay attention to the content, they are likely to ignore the message. To build credibility, notify your students before the end of the school year that you will be contacting them via text over the summer about college-related tasks. If possible, be sure that the text messages are sent from a number that includes a local area code. Use the first message to reintroduce the messaging campaign and, if possible, customize the messages so each student is ostensibly receiving the message from someone they know personally. Prompt students to save the contact information in their phone so they recognize the sender of subsequent messages, and provide a website or phone number students and families can contact if they want to verify the messaging campaign.

Fourth, build on existing relationships when possible. Across the interventions profiled, summer support staff—and the peer mentors in particular—had more success making contact when they had a prior relationship with the student. After high school graduation, your students are looking forward to the relationships that they will develop in college. Therefore, they may be less willing to establish a relationship with a person they don't know or they associate more with high school. Build on existing relationships rather than expecting students to develop a trusting relationship with an unfamiliar person.

Fifth, be at the ready. This is particularly key if reaching out to students using an approach like texting that invites an immediate response. In the case of a text campaign, messages should be sent to students when they are most likely to pay attention to them and when counselors are able to respond immediately to requests for assistance. Our own data suggests that the text outreach may have been frustrating for students when they requested assistance but did not receive a prompt response.

A related priority is to set expectations. Clarify for students when they can expect a response if they do reach out for support. For example, students may send a message over the weekend and be frustrated not to receive a response until Monday. This may be particularly true with text messages. Therefore, be explicit about when students can expect to hear back, and explain that a lag in response may be because the office is closed or staff members are not working over the weekend.

Finally, build in backup. Summer is a time when counselors and other school staff recharge from the intensity of the academic year. Counselors typically do and should enjoy vacation time during the summer. Similarly, college-aged staff members may need some flexibility to schedule additional summer work or attend classes. In planning for a summer college-going program, therefore, be sure to arrange for coverage so that support is always readily available to each college-intending student. If possible, make clear to students when their designated staff member is unavailable and who can assist them during that time.

ASSESSING YOUR IMPACT

A key strength of several of the interventions profiled in previous chapters is that they were accompanied by evaluation designs that allowed us to isolate the unique impact of summer outreach on college outcomes, separate from all the other factors that influence whether students enter and succeed in higher education. By using randomized, lottery-based studies, we were able to rigorously assess program impacts and identify which students benefited most from outreach and support. While a comprehensive discussion of research design and program evaluation is beyond the scope of this book, we recommend strongly that you build a rigorous research design into your summer initiative—as well as other programs that you pursue—so you can evaluate the quality of the implementation and the impact of the intervention on students' college-going outcomes.

With a formal evaluation your organization will be well positioned to understand whether the program is beneficial for your students, whether it represents resources well spent, and how to improve upon your program design and delivery to derive even greater benefit for subsequent cohorts of students. In evaluating your program, you will want to consider key implementation questions such as these: What share of targeted students were you able to reach? What modes of outreach were most successful for reaching students? What types of support did students seek? In what ways did program staff feel most and least prepared, supported, and successful? Also ask the key impact questions: What share of college-intending students enrolled in college in the fall? What share of students enrolled in their intended institution? To what extent do students who enroll on time persist beyond their freshman fall?

Planning for program evaluation is best done in tandem with program development, as in the first summer of uAspire's Summer College Connect (described in chapter 4). Therefore, we recommend identifying a program evaluation partner and bringing that partner on early in your planning process. Some school districts have research departments that provide in-house expertise in research and program evaluation. More typically, however, school districts and other educational agencies are lacking in this domain. If you do not have in-house research expertise, you have several options for finding it. Just as we conducted our first summer melt experiments in partnership with uAspire as doctoral students, there may be graduate students at nearby universities who would jump at the chance to partner in evaluating your intervention's implementation and impact. This type of partnership can yield a high-quality evaluation at little cost to your agency, while providing students with the opportunity to apply their skills in research design and data analysis in real-world settings.

It may be that none of the summer outreach options discussed here and in previous chapters is feasible for you, given cost and other constraints. However, it may still be beneficial to provide all of your graduates with general guidance on the summer steps that colleges typically require in order to matriculate. A sample handout for students is provided in appendix D. The key is to offer students whatever support you can during this vulnerable time and recognize that they continue to need guidance and help once they've walked across the graduation stage.

◆ ◆ ◆

CHAPTER 8

Revisiting the Road Map to College
Opportunities for Cross-Sector Collaboration

As is the case with many persistent educational inequalities, there can be a tendency among educators to blame another institution or educational sector for the summer melt problem. College transition counselors who work outside of the school system sometimes see the issue as resting with school counselors: "School guidance departments pat themselves on the back and consider their job done when kids get their acceptance letters. They don't see it as their job that kids actually go to college." Similarly, high school counselors sometimes place blame on postsecondary institutions: "Colleges aren't sensitive to the other things that are going on for students. Students have trouble keeping up with the paperwork and the different deadlines because of the bureaucratic nature of the process and the fact that they are juggling other tasks in their lives."

High school counselors and postsecondary institutions alike wrestle with their own expectations for students' families: "I've worked with students whose parents wouldn't give tax returns for financial aid applications, but if the student is going to stay on campus, the parent will have to take out a loan. This becomes an issue, as the parent is barely making ends meet. To have them take on a loan is ridiculous. These loans are not small, and they are accruing debt. Parents will be stuck with this financial obligation, which can be nerve wracking. While I can understand parents' reservation, it can be so frustrating to get parents to understand the value of education." Finally, students recognize that they are responsible for their own college plans but point to a system where the dots are not connected: "In high school, we had to see a counselor every year, but they weren't good at reinforcing what I had to get done. I wasn't prepared for the accountability and responsibility of applying to college. Students do need to be more accountable for themselves, but it would be good to understand better what the process is and who is there to help."

While some finger pointing is inevitable, educators need to collectively move beyond assigning blame and instead identify productive solutions not only to reduce summer melt, but more broadly to eliminate socioeconomic disparities in who goes to and succeeds in college. Asking the question of "who is or who should be responsible" implies that summer melt is the problem or fault of one group or institution. Instead, we propose a more productive reframing: Who *can be* (or who is well-positioned to be) responsible? What and how can different entities contribute?

Many of the summer barriers that students face derive from the complexity of the college transition process. Given this, educators have to grapple with three core questions. First, what steps can be taken to minimize the complexity of the existing process? Second, where complexity is unavoidable, what supports can be put in place to help students work through it? Third, what skills do students need in order to maximize their chances of success?

WHO CAN CONTRIBUTE TO REDUCING SUMMER MELT?

While the previous chapter provides concrete guidance to school districts and other organizations serving high school students, opportunities to address summer melt do not rest solely with the secondary education sector. Therefore, we consider how other sectors—the federal government and higher education, in particular—can contribute to this effort. In addition, we offer examples for how cross-sector collaboration may yield even further improvements through innovative solutions. After all, complex problems are often best tackled not by one entity working in isolation but by a coordinated effort that reaches across institutions and sectors.

What Can the Federal Government Do?

Implicit in the notion that "summer melt starts in February" are the challenges that students face related to financial aid. The first step in the financial aid process is submitting the FAFSA, and research has shown that increasing FAFSA completion rates has a positive impact on both college enrollment and persistence.[1] Because FAFSA completion is a key gateway to college attainment, we begin with additional steps the federal government can take to improve students' success with this critical college-going hurdle.

The U.S. Department of Education (USDOE) deserves praise for the efforts it has already made to simplify the FAFSA process. However, additional investments to more proactively support students, from initial FAFSA submission through receipt of their financial aid packages, would go a long way toward better positioning students for a successful college transition. The federal government is the ideal entity to spearhead initiatives in this arena. USDOE has full information about students' FAFSA status. It also has contact information (and the potential to collect additional information like cell phone numbers) for every FAFSA applicant—both traditional students in high school and nontraditional students who may have even less access to professional guidance with their financial aid application.

While USDOE already sends considerable communications to applicants via e-mail and postal mail, these distribution channels are far less effective for students and their families than text messaging and personalized outreach through social media. USDOE could use these technologies to send proactive reminders about students' progress throughout the financial aid application process. As discussed in chapter 5, these outreach strategies can be both automated and highly personalized, allowing for effective and efficient outreach at a large scale. For instance, USDOE could send reminders about FAFSA completion to those who have begun but not filed their FAFSA. Another set of messages could notify students who have been flagged for income verification and provide simplified guidance on how to complete the verification process. Once students are in college, messages could remind students to refile their FAFSA, and even after students leave college, USDOE could provide guidance about various loan repayment options.

While these nudges have the potential to meaningfully increase FAFSA completion rates, the financial aid process is sufficiently complex that many students will still need additional support. USDOE could therefore explore ways that interactive technologies like live chat and secure document sharing could provide FAFSA applicants with individualized assistance. These technologies could enhance the personalized guidance that USDOE already provides through its FAFSA hotline.

Finally, specific to summer melt, the federal government could use its convening power to encourage colleges and universities to adopt more transparent, standardized, and comprehensive websites that provide a one-stop summary of all the tasks that students need to complete over the summer. As discussed earlier, many colleges have websites for admitted students, but students may not be aware of them, and regardless, the tasks that students need to complete over the summer are scattered over several web pages. The USDOE created a standard and simplified format for financial aid award letters; it could do the same to guide colleges in creating and organizing their admitted-student websites.

What Can Colleges and Universities Do?

After students complete the FAFSA, the financial aid process transfers to the colleges and universities to which each student has applied. The financial aid tasks that students need to complete with each college range from verifying the information on their FAFSA, if they have been flagged to do so, to filing supplementary aid applications and interpreting and acting on their financial aid offers.

Colleges and universities are well positioned to provide outreach and guidance to prospective students about outstanding tasks that they still need to complete. Institutions have comprehensive information about whether prospective students have been asked to verify income and have properly completed that process. In addition, as colleges have moved toward robust customer relations management systems, they increasingly have detailed, real-time information about students' progress in completing various prematriculation steps.

Financial aid offices often operate with relatively small staffs, so outreach regarding the FAFSA could be handled in an automated fashion with text-messages. If text messaging is not possible, another option is e-mail, although our research indicates this is a less effective means of reaching students. Yet another option is hiring undergraduates to call students and families by phone. In this way, colleges could increase prospective students' awareness of the income verification process and support students in the institution-specific steps required to verify the information on their FAFSAs.

Colleges and universities should also adopt the USDOE Financial Aid Shopping Sheet (as discussed in chapter 3). This award letter format enables students to more easily understand their financial aid package, to distinguish grants from loans, and to compare their total aid package against the cost of attendance. The greater the number of institutions that adopt this format, the easier it will be for students to compare aid packages across institutions. This ability is clearly to students' benefit, but it is also increasingly in schools' interest to make this information transparent. The federal ratings system recently proposed by President Obama would hold colleges and universities accountable for outcomes such as whether students default on their loans—a situation that students are more likely to be in when they do not fully understand their financial aid packages or the alternative, and perhaps more affordable, college options that are available.

Even with broader adoption of the Shopping Sheet, there are sometimes additional fees that appear on tuition bills but not on financial aid award letters. These include charges like student activities or course fees, student health insurance, parking fees, and even processing fees on student loans. Colleges should itemize these fees in students' award letters, or at least include them in the total cost of attendance that they publish on the award letters. In addition, award letters should include details about whether and under what circumstances students are able to waive these fees as well as where to obtain more information about the waiver process. This would allow students to more precisely estimate what they will owe on their tuition bill months before it is due. To help students understand the credits (from financial aid) and charges on their bills, colleges and universities, with support from USDOE, could also adopt a standardized format for tuition bills analogous to the Financial Aid Shopping Sheet.

Finally, even small preenrollment expenses, like tuition deposits, housing application fees, and orientation registration charges, can pose significant challenges for students from low-income backgrounds. Where feasible, colleges should create and clearly articulate systems through which students can charge these fees forward to their tuition bills or receive fee waivers, given their low-income status, so that minor cost obstacles do not deter students from realizing their college aspirations.

Better Together?

In addition to the steps that different sectors might take to help guide students through the college transition, there are also several natural opportunities for collaborative effort across agencies and sectors. Such partnerships have the potential to greatly enhance student support.

One example of this type of cross-agency partnership is the USDOE FAFSA Completion Project. For the past several years,

USDOE has experimented with providing states and school districts with student-level information on FAFSA submission and completion status. Schools across the country are now able to receive regularly updated information on which of their students have submitted the FAFSA and which have fully completed it. In Texas, for example, counselors are provided with this information as well as whether students have been flagged for income verification after filing the FAFSA. With this data, counselors can directly target students who need assistance with the FAFSA and income verification. While data systems are still being developed for districts to receive and disseminate this student-level information, schools can, at the very least, track their students' FAFSA progress with school-level completion data that is already publicly available.[2]

There is also promise in stronger collaborations between the secondary and postsecondary education sectors, with the goal of creating a more deliberate handoff of students from high schools to colleges and universities. In many school districts, the majority of college-aspiring students intend to enroll in one of a relatively small number of nearby colleges and universities. For example, the vast majority of college-intending graduates from the Albuquerque Public Schools plan to continue their education at either the University of New Mexico (UNM) or the Community College of New Mexico (CNM). Recently, the Albuquerque Public Schools implemented a college-going intervention in collaboration with these two postsecondary institutions. School district counselors were employed through the summer months by the Albuquerque schools, but were stationed on the UNM and CNM campuses rather than the district high schools. The counselors reached out to students who had been admitted to the institution where they were stationed to offer help with summer tasks, in much the same way uAspire advisors and Fulton County counselors did, as profiled in chapter 4. By working from the college instead of the high school site, counselors were able to gain deeper insight into both the tasks for which students were responsible and the college-based resources that were available to help them. Having counselors act on behalf of students' intended college or university generated the added benefit of making the students feel their college was invested in their success and wanted them to make it to campus. This is but one example; postsecondary systems and the secondary schools that feed into them could collaborate on devising additional strategies to support students during the college transition.

As discussed in previous chapters, another challenge for some students is a lack of parental support for college plans. This stance may derive from parents' lack of understanding of the processes required to get to college or of the benefits that a college education can offer. We encourage educational systems to identify opportunities for partnership with local employers, unions, faith-based communities, and other groups to which parents belong in order to effectively communicate with them about the benefits of college, options for college financing, and how to support their children's college aspirations.

We encourage other opportunities for creative collaboration to solve summer challenges that students face. For example, could high schools collaborate with area businesses to sponsor students' travel for orientation and the start of the academic year? Might colleges call on their alumni networks to provide such transportation directly? While low in cost, this symbolic gesture of supporting a student's start to college may have powerful impacts. The particular types of collaboration that are possible are likely to be community specific, yet are also apt to be limited only by the creativity and imagination of educators and community members. Communities should ask how they can help improve postsecondary outcomes among their college-intending students and think creatively about what they might accomplish through collaboration and partnership.

What Students Need

Even with the efforts called for above, many aspects of the college-going process remain too complex for adolescents to navigate effectively on their own. Therefore, all students would benefit from having a college-going "champion"—a knowledgeable adult who can guide them from their initial exploration of college through to matriculation. Middle- and upper-income students typically have college-going champions in their own parents. It is less clear who can serve in this role for lower-income students, especially when they are the first in their family to go to college. For these students, a champion could instead be a teacher, a school counselor, a faith-community leader, an athletic coach, a member of a community-based organization, or a near-age peer. Even when students are informed that help is available, they rarely seek it out. Students' champions should therefore proactively reach out, whether by phone, Facebook, text, or in person, to check in with the student, inquire about progress and roadblocks, and provide support and encouragement for moving forward. This is the approach taken by iMentor, the nonprofit organization discussed in chapter 5 that pairs low-income students in New York City with a mentor to support them, from college exploration through to matriculation and beyond.

To be clear, this is not meant to imply that students are free from responsibility or that another person should complete key college-going steps on the student's behalf. Instead, educators, counselors, and other college-going champions should help students develop the college know-how as well as noncognitive skills, such as self-sufficiency and self-advocacy, that will position them for collegiate success. This is the orientation that uAspire takes in all of its student-support initiatives, as discussed in chapter 4. As one college transition coach said, "We need to help [students] learn that there is a support network beyond just one or two people." To work toward this goal, for example, this coach organized an event for her high school students where directors of different offices— such as financial aid, the registrar, billing, academic support—from an area college came and talked to groups of her students. This helped students to see that the people at these offices are accessible and willing to help. Because students are sometimes confused about where to go for help at their college or intimidated about interacting with unfamiliar staff, this type of event can help to break down barriers and enhance students' capacity to seek out help independently.

Hand-in-hand with the ability to self-advocate are the soft skills of communication. As one college transition counselor explained, the students with whom she works often lack these skills: "Students graduate from high school and they feel like high school prepared them academically. But after they graduate, then what? Something as small as calling a financial aid office to ask about financial aid poses problems for students. They don't have those soft skills; they don't know what to say. They may know what they need, but they don't know how to ask for [it]. When I work with students, I try to help them articulate what they need. Sometimes I make a call on behalf of a student in order to model the behavior—be polite, have your ID and social security numbers ready. I coach students on how to interact. School doesn't prepare students with these critical social skills. They simply don't know what to say." Students need proactive encouragement to reach out for help and ask questions. They also need opportunities to have these behaviors modeled and coached, as described in the preceding quote.

Finally, students need support in strengthening their financial literacy. They should be literate in topics specific to financial aid, such as understanding net price versus sticker price, grant aid versus loan aid, and total aid versus the cost of attendance, but also have broader skills in budgeting and money management. Students must be able to budget for ongoing expenses, such as books, transportation, and unanticipated course or activity fees. In addition, students need to understand what their financial aid package is likely to be for the duration of their college career so they can anticipate how they'll pay for subsequent years.

A point worth emphasizing is that many students—and not just those from low-income backgrounds—lack the skills of financial literacy, communication, and self-advocacy. A critical difference is that, whereas well-informed and proactive parents can compensate for their child's inexperience in these areas, students from low-income families often do not have the benefit of this parental safety net. For students from low-income backgrounds, who often have to navigate the transition to college independently, success in making it to and through college may depend on whether they can acquire these competencies at an earlier age than their peers with more family-based supports.

A PERSONALIZED "ROAD MAP" FOR COLLEGE

The focus of this book is the phenomenon of summer melt. Yet the implications of this body of research extend well beyond the months between high school graduation and initial college enrollment. The summer steps to which students must attend are a component of a longer, complex, multistage and multiyear process of college exploration, application, selection, and transition that low-income and first-generation students often struggle to navigate. The phases of this process that precede and follow the summer deserve equal attention to ensure that an increasingly diverse group of students not only gains admission to college but also earns a college degree.

Our conversations with students and counselors highlight that, while most students aspire to college, this multistage process is often quite murky. This is not for lack of information. Many high schools post or distribute brochures describing what students need to do to apply. Similarly, just about every college has a webpage enumerating the tasks that admitted students need to complete over the summer. Nevertheless, the impact of these resources may be limited because they are often complicated, impersonal, and distributed through ineffective channels. Even when information is available online and in more interactive formats, the volume of factors students need to consider is often so overwhelming that they have a hard time knowing where to focus their attention. Instead, students need a stronger signal that the information is relevant to them and support in interpreting how it pertains to their own circumstances and life goals.

More broadly, it is not sufficient to passively make information available for students. When students were simply informed at the start of the summer that college transition support was available, virtually no students took advantage of it. Instead, personalized outreach prompted students to take up and benefit from summer counseling. Policy makers and educators should provide college-aspiring students with personalized and timely prompts, encouragement, and, if possible, feedback regarding the completion of each key milestone. This communication helps keep students motivated and oriented on their college path. In providing personalized prompts to students, it would also be possible to notify family members, educators, or another designated champion when a key task has been or still needs to be completed.

In short, many students would benefit from more deliberate guidance through the college-going process. However, it is not sufficient to provide static direction at a single point in time. Instead, students should receive ongoing support, with regular feedback about their progress. Ideally, this support would capitalize on innovative technology—such as text-based outreach and web-based information and planning tools—but would also enable students to obtain guidance from a caring and knowledgeable adult. In our view, both types of support are needed to help students navigate the college-going terrain.

We liken our call for improved, step-by-step support for students to the navigation revolution. Just a few years ago, most of us were still using fold-up maps stuck in our glove compartments to figure out the best route from one place to another. For the directionally challenged among us, this wasn't an easy task. Paper maps can become outdated quickly and don't provide information on new options or on potential barriers such as detours, construction sites, and accidents.

Interactive apps have radically changed navigation. Rather than planning each turn of your route from beginning to end, now all you have to do is tell your GPS where you want to go. It can guide you there step-by-step. It can provide route options and, in real time, highlight the literal roadblocks associated with a given path. The apps are so sophisticated that they can even reroute you in real time to compensate for any wrong turns or unforeseen barriers.

Thus, to cover all the ground in students' journey from high school to college, we need to focus on strategies to help them navigate college consideration, application, and selection as well as transition.

College Entrance Exams: An Important First Step

One of their first steps is to complete college entrance exams. At many colleges and universities, the SAT or ACT is required as part of the application. Even among colleges that do not require them, students who score sufficiently well can use these exams to qualify as college ready and therefore place out of remedial coursework.

But there is an added benefit to taking a college entrance exam, and further, to taking it prior to senior year in high school: not only can students send their scores to colleges in which they are interested, but colleges (which purchase students' names directly from ACT or the College Board) can use the information to recruit students. Simply by taking a three-hour exam, students may receive information from several institutions, and thus be exposed to a range of postsecondary possibilities that might change their perception of themselves as college material. In recognition of the importance of taking college entrance exams, at the time of this writing, fourteen states and several other school districts have implemented universal, school-day SAT or ACT for all students during their junior year of high school.[3]

Absent these types of policies, low-income and first-generation students currently are less likely to take the exams. And those who do are more likely to take college entrance exams later in their high school trajectory and less likely to retake them to improve upon their initial score.[4] Encouragingly, research reveals that universal, school-day testing and other test-encouragement policies lead to improvements in a range of outcomes, such as the number of colleges to which students apply and whether students eventually enroll in college.[5] Therefore, proactive college information and advising should help students identify taking a college entrance exam as a first step. Students may benefit from timely reminders to register and prepare for the test, to take advantage of fee waivers for which they qualify, and to organize transportation for the day of the exam. Upon taking the SAT or ACT, students may need support to interpret their scores, to use their scores to identify potential colleges and universities, and to decide whether retaking the exam would be worthwhile. For example, certain college systems use an SAT benchmark to determine college readiness. Students should receive feedback on whether they have come close to, met, or surpassed benchmarks for the schools to which they plan to apply. For students who have just missed a benchmark, educators could send proactive advice to study for and retake the exam.

Matching Schools and Students

Next, a growing body of research indicates that students often apply to and attend colleges and universities that are not well-matched to their abilities or resources.[6] For example, as many as half of all academically accomplished, low-income students who could attend well-resourced institutions with high graduation rates and strong academic and social supports instead matriculate at institutions with fewer supports and low rates of college completion. In other cases, students choose institutions that don't provide them with sufficient funding, even net of federal and other financial aid, for their financial circumstances.

Therefore, students and families should receive personalized information that identifies affordable college options that are aligned to the combination of their academic skills, extracurricular and social interests, and future goals. In the same way that we sent college-intending high school graduates personalized text reminders of summer tasks to be completed, high school juniors and seniors may benefit from personalized information about colleges that are well-matched to their abilities, are affordable, and have high success rates. Caroline Hoxby and Sarah Turner pioneered this approach in their Expanding College Opportunities (ECO) project, through which they mailed high-achieving, low-income students packets of customized information about high-quality colleges to which they had a good chance of being admitted.[7] The College Board is currently expanding ECO-style efforts to a broader range of students. For example, recognizing that students are more likely to reach their college goals if they apply to multiple institutions, the College Board has undertaken a campaign to encourage students to apply to "Four or More" colleges or universities.[8] Students should be counseled in these and other application strategies and best practices.

Applying for and Understanding Financial Aid

After submitting college applications, many students and families would benefit from guidance to complete the FAFSA and other financial aid applications specific to their locality. For example, New York State has its Tuition Assistance Program, which provides up to $5,000 in grant-based tuition assistance to qualified students, and several U.S. cities run Promise scholarship programs to provide financial aid to qualified college goers. Nonetheless, a substantial share of low-income and first-generation students may not understand the benefits of completing the FAFSA or know that these supports exist. Students who start the FAFSA may not realize that their application is incomplete or that they have been flagged for income verification. Applying for financial aid is also a time-sensitive process, as states, colleges, and universities hold firm priority deadlines for application filing.

The USDOE has taken substantial steps to simplify the FAFSA process. In addition, privately funded programs like College Goal Sunday assist students and families across the country in completing the FAFSA.[9] Fortunately, the USDOE's FAFSA Completion Project can now tell many high schools whether their seniors have started or completed the FAFSA. While secondary schools do some proactive outreach to students based on this information, districts and students alike may benefit from automated tools that can inform students of their FAFSA status. This information could be provided to students together with prompts to seek additional support from local organizations that help with the FAFSA and with a reminder that income verification is sometimes required after FAFSA completion.

The final stop before high school graduation on students' college-going journey should be to review the financial aid award letters from the colleges and universities to which they have been accepted. Students should receive guidance to differentiate grant aid from loan assistance, weigh the aid package against the total cost of attendance at each institution, and identify possible sources of additional funding, either from the federal government or from local scholarship programs. As with the FAFSA completion supports, students should be connected to community resources that can help them review their award letters.

A Road Map to Matriculation

After students select their intended institution, the college should supply institution-specific matriculation guidance, enumerating the key tasks to be completed over the summer—placement tests, orientation, housing paperwork, tuition payment plans, promissory note signing, logistics for traveling to campus, and others. As with our text message outreach, this guidance should provide the deadlines for each step and, importantly, where students can turn if they need help accomplishing or affording these tasks. Colleges and universities could assume responsibility to organize this information in a user-friendly, digestible fashion.

As we have emphasized throughout the book, the pathway from college consideration to successful enrollment requires students to engage in multiple tasks, take in and interpret a great deal of information, and make a series of weighty decisions. Encouragingly, there are many excellent resources, websites, and web-based tools to inform and support students throughout this transition. Yet, the many stages of the college journey together with the complexity and volume of information available can be dizzying, particularly for students and families with little experience in the college-going process. Layer on top of this the variety of supports that are available in some communities, and it is easy to see how students and families may lack a clear sense of what is required when, and which entities and organizations can provide needed assistance. Therefore, in addition to personalized guidance for these students, we advocate for a "road map" tool focused on college access that can break down the stages of the college-going process and the associated key information into digestible, bite-sized chunks with which students and families can engage and thus make more informed decisions. Such a tool could incorporate the technological capacity to provide regular reminders of upcoming tasks, just as your GPS reminds you that your next turn is coming in a half mile. The tool could also include a counselor-facing dashboard to provide easy-to-digest information on how students are progressing on the road to college. This feature may be particularly useful for the counselors, who are often juggling multiple responsibilities at the same time that they are trying to guide students to well-matched colleges.

Currently, several organizations are developing tools that bring the idea of a personalized college road map to life. Specific to summer melt, for example, College Bound St. Louis is developing an interactive web-based tool to guide school counselors and students along the path from high school graduation to college matriculation. Lisa Orden Zarin, CEO of College Bound, describes the tool, MySummer GPS, as "the Turbo Tax of college access" because of the way it guides users through the summer with a sequence of simplified prompts while adapting to the information they provide in response. Similar tools were recently featured at an Education Datapalooza organized by the White House and the USDOE and have garnered considerable interest for their potential to provide students, parents, and school personnel with highly customized guidance on the college process. Of course, the development of such tools should be coupled with efforts to rigorously understand how they are used by students, their families, and other supporting adults to maximize their use and contribution to improved college

outcomes. As discussed in chapters 4 through 6, lottery-based studies, where access to the tool is rolled out in phases, would provide
the best opportunity to understand their impact and potential.

In addition to focusing on the steps that culminate in college enrollment, we can apply the lessons from mitigating summer melt
to ensure that students who make it to college stay and earn a
degree. Of students who enroll in college, nearly half fail to obtain a degree (either two- or four-year) within six years.[10] Addressing prematriculation summer challenges will position students for
a better start to their college careers. Once on campus, however,
colleges and universities should continue to provide students with
timely, proactive, and personalized information to help them progress toward their degree. This outreach should focus both on key
academic benchmarks and available tutoring and advising as well
as on more procedural tasks, like FAFSA renewal, that are instrumental to students' persistence in college.

Even the most well-connected and perseverant students are not
impervious to challenges that can derail their plans. Alex Chewning, the director of research and evaluation at uAspire, shared the
story of a student who, shortly before his senior year in college,
realized that he could not afford the final year of college bills. As
a result, he reluctantly decided that he needed to withdraw from
college for the semester. This was a student who had worked with
uAspire for a number of years and, as a result, was knowledgeable about both the challenges surrounding college affordability
as well as the resources available to help students meet financial
gaps. He was a strong student and passionate about his studies,
but nonetheless found himself in the position of having to take
time off just months from his expected graduation. As Chewning reflected, this student's situation was "unbelievable, really, and
paints yet another picture of just how tenuous college plans are—at
any given moment—when there is no financial safety net . . . Each
postsecondary year—with its new award letter and new crop of
bills—represents its own new battlefield for too many low-income
students."

CONCLUSION

◆ ◆ ◆

Lessons from Summer Melt

As the experiences of the profiled students illustrate, the summer after high school is not the carefree time that American culture has long portrayed it to be. Nonetheless, the summer *can* be a period of renewed hope and opportunity. Though college-intending high school graduates encounter various obstacles during the summer months, they are responsive to the offer of professional assistance and, with this help, often matriculate successfully. The summer interventions we profile are low cost compared to many other attempts to improve college access, but nonetheless have generated substantial increases in both college enrollment and persistence.

Several important lessons emerge from these studies. First, the challenges that students face over the summer months are surmountable. Each year there are thousands of low-income high school graduates who have already overcome many hurdles in the college path and who, with a small amount of additional support in the eleventh hour, would be well-positioned for postsecondary entry. Admittedly, the summer transition is but one piece of the larger puzzle of increasing college access and success for disadvantaged students. Policy makers must continue to invest in strategies to mitigate chronic sources of inequality in postsecondary readiness and attainment. Helping students navigate preenrollment hurdles can make a considerable dent in these disparities. Further, even for those students who do not succumb to summer melt, the challenges that they face prior to enrollment can lead them to limp across the starting line. Helping students address challenges they encounter in the summer can help them get out of the gate better positioned for the marathon of their college careers.

A related lesson is that students' struggles to overcome stumbling blocks prior to matriculation don't necessarily reflect their ability to succeed in postsecondary education. Prematriculation tasks pose challenges for adolescents across the socioeconomic spectrum. As one uAspire advisor noted, summer outreach and support essentially "fills in for what middle-class parents do with their children every day." Providing additional support to first-generation students during these months clears the way for them to transition to and succeed in academic and social environments that more closely mirror their high school experiences than do the summer tasks they have to complete. In fact, building students' capacity to complete summer tasks independently can have a lasting impact. Enhancing students' ability to handle financial and procedural tasks and to proactively seek out assistance is likely to pay dividends throughout their college careers, and may underlie the lasting impacts of summer outreach on students' persistence in college. For all of these reasons, addressing summer melt and paving the often rocky transition from high school to postsecondary education may be a powerful strategy for narrowing socioeconomic gaps in college access and success.

More broadly, the barriers that students encounter during the summer after high school offer a window into the challenges that surround longstanding efforts to remedy inequalities in college access and success. Starting early in high school and continuing through college, students must navigate a long sequence of complicated processes and complex information that can hinder their ability to make well-informed decisions about their postsecondary options. Too frequently, students from economically disadvantaged backgrounds lack access to professional guidance to navigate these decisions. As a result, they often choose paths to and through higher education that are not well matched to their interests and abilities. The strategies that have mitigated summer melt—providing personalized and simplified information and helping students connect to college and financial aid experts—could be extended both earlier and later in students' educational trajectories. These investments, which can be made at a local and national level and by both the secondary and higher education sectors, are essential to support an increasingly diverse population of students to realize their college aspirations. Public investments in higher education are substantial. In 2012, for example, state and local governments allocated over $80 billion to the financing of public higher education.[1] And the economic and nonpecuniary returns to higher education are large and continue to grow. Individuals with a college degree now earn over $15,000 more *each year* than individuals with only some college.[2] Yet socioeconomic inequalities in college access and success have only widened over time, with fewer than 10 percent of students in the lowest-income quartile earning a bachelor's degree by age twenty-five.[3] For all of the public dollars devoted to higher education, shouldn't we expect success rates greater than these? Providing students with better supports to navigate the transition to college and, in turn, positioning them for a stronger start in college may be one piece of solving this longstanding puzzle.

Our own collaboration to investigate summer melt began primarily with more arms-length, quantitative approaches to assess the prevalence of the phenomenon in a variety of educational settings. We then spent several years in partnership with school districts and community-based organizations designing and implementing various strategies to mitigate summer melt. It was in writing this book, however, that we had the opportunity to really roll up our sleeves and interact more personally with many students who had their hard-fought college plans seriously threatened by the many challenges that emerged during their transition to college. We have found inspiration in these students' resolve to achieve their college dreams and in the commitment of the caring and supportive adults who played a critical role in guiding them through this often turbulent time. Despite the many great schools and organizations that now invest in summer supports, our work is unfinished. The aggregate data tells us that too many students across the country still struggle to make it over the hurdles they encounter in the months following high school graduation. Our hope is that this book, and the summer challenges of the students we profile, will catalyze an even broader array of supports at the local, state, and national levels to ensure that more college-aspiring students successfully transition to postsecondary education.

◆ ◆ ◆

Sample College Transition Cheat Sheet

In our summer melt interventions we collaborated with our partner organizations to develop college cheat sheets for the colleges and universities most frequently attended by graduates from those sites. The cheat sheets summarized in one page all of the tasks students needed to complete in order to successfully matriculate in college. College advisors reported that they frequently used these cheat sheets when meeting individually with students.

Bunker Hill Community College (www.bhcc.mass.edu)

Quick Tips:

★ Log on to the BHCC web portal to access important financial aid and other information: http://onlineservices.bhcc.mass.edu (see below for log-in info)

★ Complete FAFSA (school code: 011210) and apply for financial aid at BHCC if you haven't already

★ Complete required Accuplacer tests as soon as possible (see below)

★ Register for a Start Smart Orientation session (see info below)

Apply	◆ Complete online application at www.bhcc.mass.edu or submit application to Admissions & Registration Desk (main lobby of B Building); Pay application fee ◆ Follow-up: Submit high school diploma, high school transcript, or GED
Financial aid	◆ Complete FAFSA and submit to BHCC as soon as possible (school code: 011210). ◆ Submit the FAFSA by **August 1** for award notification prior to start of classes. ◆ You may contact the financial aid office at finaid@bhcc.mass.edu or call at 617-228-2275.
Testing	◆ All students are required to take the Accuplacer Computerized Placement Test in math, English and reading. ◆ Testing takes place at the BHCC Campus, Room B118. You can contact the Assessment Center at 617-228-2468. ◆ The Accuplacer is available on a walk-in basis. Be sure to bring a government-issued ID with you. ◆ For more info: http://www.bhcc.mass.edu/inside/126
Computing	◆ To access your online account, go to http://onlineservices.bhcc.mass.edu and click on "Current Students," then click on "What's my User ID?" to obtain your username using either your social security number or Student ID number. ◆ Once you've created your User ID, you can reset your password by clicking on "What's my password?"
Term bill	◆ Pay tuition and fees by July 11 ◆ Make payment arrangements prior to registration. Options include: (1) Paying term bill in full, (2) having pending financial aid award from BHCC, (3) submitting third party commitment letter or purchase order to Student Payment Office, or (4) creating a BHCC payment plan online (1st payment & $35 fee due at time of plan creation). To enroll in the payment plan, go here http://bhcc.mass.edu/inside/1964 and follow "Simple Steps to Enroll in the Payment Plan." ◆ **You may be able to waive BHCC's health insurance in favor of your current insurance, potentially saving you hundreds of dollars.** For more info: http://onlineservices.bhcc.mass.edu ◆ Cost of Attendance at BHCC (includes tuition, fees, books, transportation): $5,184
Orientation and registration	◆ Attend the 5-hour BHCC Start Smart Orientation with sessions throughout June, the last of which is June 27. However, more dates will become available later in the summer so check back to see the new dates and register here: www.bhcc.mass.edu/startsmart ◆ You must have taken the Accuplacer exam by the beginning of your orientation session. ◆ Arrive at orientation with a valid government issued photo ID, your username and password for the portal (see above) and a copy of your health insurance card. ◆ The first day of classes for the Fall 2012 semester is September 4.

◆ ◆ ◆

Sample High School Exit Survey

In several of our summer interventions we relied on high school exit surveys to capture whether students intended to go to college as of high school graduation, and if so, where they planned to enroll. We also relied on exit surveys to collect students' and parents' cell phone numbers for our text message interventions. The example in appendix B is from the Dallas Independent School District.

Dallas school counselors want to help make your postsecondary plans a reality!

This summer Dallas counselors will be reaching out to students and their families to offer help with the final steps in the college-going process, and to help you work through any challenges that come up in making your postsecondary plans happen. So that we can get in touch with you, please provide the following updated contact information.

> **Students who submit complete exit surveys will be entered into a raffle for a free iPad!**

_____   _____   _____
LAST NAME (PRINT)   FIRST NAME (PRINT)   ID#

_____   _____
YOUR CELL PHONE #   *YOUR* EMAIL ADDRESS (PRINT)

_____
NAME OF PARENT/GUARDIAN YOU PREFER WE CONTACT (PRINT)

_____   _____
PARENT/GUARDIAN'S CELL PHONE #   *PARENT/GUARDIAN'S* EMAIL ADDRESS (PRINT)

Please also let us know what you plan to do after high school graduation:

☐ Attend a *four-year* college/university *in Texas*:
   ☐ University of North Texas   ☐ Texas Woman's University   ☐ Texas A&M, Commerce
   ☐ UT – Arlington   ☐ UT – Austin   ☐ UT – Dallas   ☐ Other:_____

☐ Attend a *four-year* college/university *out of state*:
   Name of college _____
   Location (city/state): _____

If you plan to attend a four-year college/university, did you pay a deposit to enroll at (or get a deposit fee waiver from) your intended college/university?
   __Yes   __No   __Don't Know

☐ Attend a *two-year* college:
   ☐ DCCCD   ☐ Other: _____

☐ Attend a *Trade School*:
   Name _____
   Location (city/state): _____

☐ Enlist into *Military Service*:
   Military Branch _____

☐ *Work full-time* (list type of work/place of employment):

_____

☐ *Unsure of plans*

Approximately how many times during senior year did you meet individually with a school counselor to discuss your postsecondary plans?
   __0   __1 – 3   __4 – 6   __more than 6 times

Text Message Templates for Students and Parents

In our summer texting campaign we developed a set of common message templates that we sent out to all students and where possible, their parents. These templates addressed the key tasks that students needed to complete in order to successfully matriculate in college. The bracketed fields below indicate where we personalized messages to students.

1. **MESSAGE PURPOSE:** Introductory message

   GENERIC MESSAGE TO STUDENT:
   Hi [STUDENT NM], this is [PROMINENT PERSON]. We want to help you w/ college! Stay tuned for key summer To Dos. Save this #, you can txt us for help!

   GENERIC MESSAGE TO PARENT:
   Hi [PARENT NM], this is [PROMINENT PERSON]. We want to help [STUDENT NM] w/ college! Stay tuned for key summer To Dos. Save this #, you can txt for help.

2. MESSAGE PURPOSE: Have students log on to their web portals

GENERIC MESSAGE TO STUDENT:
Hi [STUDENT NM]! Log on to the [INST ABREV] web portal for key info: [TINYURL WEBPORTAL] Need login info? Visit www.scope2012.org. Need help? Reply MTG.

GENERIC MESSAGE TO PARENT:
Remind [STUDENT NM] to log on to the [INST ABREV] web portal for key info: [TINYURL WEBPORTAL] Need login info? Visit www.scope2012.org. Need help? Reply MTG.

3. MESSAGE PURPOSE: Have students ask questions about FAFSA or financial aid award letter

GENERIC MESSAGE TO STUDENT:
Hi [STUDENT NM]! Need help w/ the FAFSA? Questions about your fin. aid award letter, or need more aid? Reply MTG to meet w/ a [DISTRICT] counselor.

GENERIC MESSAGE TO PARENT:
Does [STUDENT NM] need help w/ the FAFSA? Questions about the fin. aid award, or need more aid? Reply MTG to meet w/ a [DISTRICT] counselor.

4. MESSAGE PURPOSE: Have students sign up for orientation

GENERIC MESSAGE TO STUDENT:
Hi [STUDENT NM]! Have you signed up for the [INST ABREV] orientation? Last one is [FN ORIEN]. Need to register? [TINYURL REGI PAGE] Need help? Reply MTG to talk w/ a counselor.

GENERIC MESSAGE TO PARENT:
Has [STUDENT NM] signed up for the [INST ABREV] orientation? Last one is [FN ORIEN]. Need to register? [TINYURL REGI PAGE] Need help? Reply MTG to talk w/ a counselor.

5. MESSAGE PURPOSE: Inquire whether students' college plans have changed

GENERIC MESSAGE TO STUDENT:
Hi [STUDENT'S NAME]! Still planning to attend [INSTITUTION ABBREVIATION] or have your plans changed? Need a Plan B? Reply MTG to meet with a [DISTRICT] counselor.

GENERIC MESSAGE TO PARENT:
Is [STUDENT'S NAME] still planning to attend [INSTITUTION ABBREVIA-TION] or have their plans changed? Need a Plan B? Reply MTG to meet with a [DISTRICT] counselor.

6. **MESSAGE PURPOSE:** Reminder about tuition bill release

GENERIC MESSAGE TO STUDENT:
Hi [STUDENT'S NAME]! The [INSTITUTION ABBREVIATION] tuition bill is coming soon! Need info about tuition payments? [TINYURL CUSTOMIZED TO EACH INSTITUTION'S TUITION PAYMENT PAGE] Need help with the bill? Reply MTG to this msg.

GENERIC MESSAGE TO PARENT:
Hi [PARENT'S NAME]! The [INSTITUTION ABBREVIATION] tuition bill is coming soon! Need info about tuition payments? [TINYURL CUSTOMIZED TO EACH INSTITUTION'S TUITION PAYMENT PAGE] Need help with the bill? Reply MTG to this msg.

7. **MESSAGE PURPOSE:** Have students take placement tests

GENERIC MESSAGE TO STUDENT:
Hi [STUDENT NM]! Remember to take the [INST ABREV] placement tests or get an exemption. Need info? [TINYURL PLACEMENT] Need help? Reply MTG to this msg.

GENERIC MESSAGE TO PARENT:
Has [STUDENT NM] taken the [INST ABREV] placement tests or gotten an exemption? Need info? [TINYURL PLACEMENT] Need help? Reply MTG to this msg.

8. **MESSAGE PURPOSE:** Let students know they may be required to have health insurance

GENERIC MESSAGE TO STUDENT:
Hi [STUDENT'S NAME]! [INSTITUTION] may require you to have health in-surance. Need info on health care options/costs? [TINYURL CUSTOMIZED TO EACH INSTITUTION'S HEALTH CARE PAGE] Need help? Reply MTG.

GENERIC MESSAGE TO PARENT:
[STUDENT'S NAME] may be required to have health insurance at [INSTITU-TION]. Need info on health care options/costs? [TINYURL CUSTOMIZED TO EACH INSTITUTION'S HEALTH CARE PAGE] Need help? Reply MTG.

9. MESSAGE PURPOSE: check in text

GENERIC MESSAGE TO STUDENT:
Hi [STUDENT NM]! How's the college planning going? Need help with any-thing? Reply MTG. For info on key tasks to complete: www.scope2012.org

GENERIC MESSAGE TO PARENT:
Hi [PARENT'S NAME]! How's [STUDENT NM]'s college planning going? Need help with anything? Reply MTG. For info on key tasks to complete: www.scope2012.org

10. MESSAGE PURPOSE: Reminder about tuition bills

GENERIC MESSAGE TO STUDENT:
Hi! The [INST ABREV] tuition bill is due [TUIT DUE]. Need info about tuition payment options? [TINYURL TUITIONPG] Need help with the bill? Reply MTG.

GENERIC MESSAGE TO PARENT:
Hi! The [INST ABREV] tuition bill is due [TUIT DUE]. Need info about tuition payments? [TINYURL TUITIONPG] Need help with the bill? Reply MTG to this msg.

11. MESSAGE PURPOSE: reminder about the first day of the semester and move-in date

GENERIC MESSAGE TO STUDENT:
Hi [STUDENT NM]! Can you believe the first day of classes at [INST ABREV] is [1st DAY CLASS] and move-in day is [MOVE-IN]?! We hope you have a great year!

GENERIC MESSAGE TO STUDENT IF THERE IS NO MOVE-IN DATE:
Hi [STUDENT NM]! Can you believe the first day of classes at [INST ABREV] is [1st DAY CLASS]?! We hope you have a great year!

GENERIC MESSAGE TO PARENT:
Can you believe [STUDENT NM]'s first day of classes at [INST ABREV] is [1st DAY CLASSES] and move-in day is [MOVE-IN]?! We hope [STUDENT NM] has a great year!

GENERIC MESSAGE TO PARENT IF THERE IS NO MOVE-IN DATE:
Can you believe [STUDENT NM]'s first day of classes at [INST ABREV] is [1st DAY CLASS]?! We hope [STUDENT NM] has a great year!

◆ ◆ ◆

Overview of Required
College Matriculation Tasks

In our summer melt interventions we notified all students that counseling assistance would be available during the summer if they needed help with any aspect of their transition to college. In some sites we also distributed one-page documents, like the one below, that summarized the key tasks that students needed to complete in order to successfully matriculate.

Nine steps to making your college plans a reality!

There are important steps that need to be completed over the summer for you to be able to enroll in the fall. The tasks listed below are common to most colleges, but you should check your acceptance materials or contact your college to see if there are other tasks specific to your college. To find out how to complete any of the tasks below at your college, call your admissions office or try a Google search for each task. For instance, if you are attending the University of New Mexico and want to appeal your financial aid, Google "University of New Mexico financial aid appeal."

1. **CONTACT A SCHOOL COUNSELOR IF YOU NEED HELP OVER THE SUMMER!** Counselors will be working this summer to help you with any challenges that arise. On your city's web page within the SCOPE 2012 site, you can find the email address for the counselor(s) helping graduates from your high school.

2. **Log on to your college's personalized web site:** Most colleges now provide a website, named something like my.collegename.edu, where you can check your financial aid status and other important deadlines.
   • Your username and password were probably sent with your acceptance packet or in a separate letter/email. If you can't find your username and password, contact your school's admissions office.

3. **Check the status of your financial aid:**
   • Complete the FAFSA and apply for aid if you haven't already.
   • Check your most recent award letter and your personalized web site to see whether there are additional steps you need to take to apply for aid.
   • If you are considering an appeal, contact your financial aid office to ask how to appeal.

4. **Register for your college's orientation:** Many colleges now hold required summer orientations for all first-year students.

- Register ASAP, since many colleges hold their orientations early in summer.
- Check what documents you are required to bring with you to orientation.

5. **Check whether you need to complete placement testing before the start of the semester or before orientation:** Colleges often require placement tests in math, reading, and writing. Some colleges do these tests at Orientation; others require you to do the tests online or on campus beforehand.

6. **Complete any housing forms, if your college offers housing:** Most colleges require you to pay a housing deposit and complete a housing form in order to be eligible for on-campus housing. Some colleges have limited housing, so do this ASAP.

7. **Check when term bills are issued and when they are due:** Talk with your counselor about how to pay whatever balance is left after your financial aid award. You can also talk with your counselor and your parents about the possibility of setting up a tuition payment plan.

8. **Check your college's policy around health insurance:** Colleges have different rules for which students are required to have health insurance, and whether students are automatically enrolled in the college's student health insurance plan.
   - Check your college's requirements ASAP, since the college health insurance can be costly.
   - If you already have qualifying insurance, you may be able to apply for a health insurance waiver.

9. **Submit other required paperwork and documentation:**
   - Your college will expect to receive proof of your high school completion. Submit your final high school transcript and an official indication of your graduation to your college's admissions office.
   - Especially if you're expecting to live on campus, your school's health services will require evidence of your immunizations. Submit immunization records to health services.

NOTES

INTRODUCTION

1. Benjamin L. Castleman and Lindsay C. Page, "A Trickle or a Torrent? Understanding the Extent of Summer 'Melt' Among College-Intending High School Graduates," *Social Science Quarterly* 95, no. 1 (March 2014), http://onlinelibrary.wiley.com/doi/10.1111/ssqu.12032/pdf.

2. Chris Matthews, Korynn Schooley, and Niveen Vosler, "Proposal for a Summer Transition Program to Increase FCS College-Going Rates" (unpublished report, Fulton County Schools, Fulton County, GA). Lindsay Daugherty, "An Evaluation of Summer Link, A Counseling Program to Facilitate College-Going" (paper presented at the fall conference of the Association of Policy Analysis and Management, Baltimore, MD, November 2011).

3. The phrase "summer flood" was originally coined by Professor Karen Arnold of Boston College.

4. Karen C. Arnold, Shezwae Fleming, Mario DeAnda, Benjamin L. Castleman, and Katherine L. Wartman, "The Summer Flood: The Invisible Gap Among Low-Income Students," *Thought and Action*, Fall 2009, 23–34.

5. Jennifer Iriti and William Bickel, "Promises Not Yet Realized: Those Who Could But Don't Use Available Place-Based Scholarship Funds" (Evaluation for Learning Project, University of Pittsburgh Learning Research and Development Center, 2011).

6. Karen C. Arnold, Benjamin L. Castleman, Alexandra Chewning, and Lindsay C. Page, "Advisor and Student Experiences of Summer Support for College-Intending, Low-Income High School Graduates" (paper presented at the fall conference of the Association for the Study of Higher Education, St. Louis, MO, November 2013).

7. Executive Office of the President, "Increasing College Opportunity for Low-Income Students," 2014, http://www.whitehouse.gov/sites/default/files/docs/white_house_report_on_increasing_college_opportunity_for_low-income_students.pdf.

8. The National Student Clearinghouse (NSC) is a nonprofit organization that houses student degree and enrollment information for colleges and universities in the United States. At the time of our writing, approximately 3,500 colleges and universities participated in the NSC. www.studentclearinghouse.org.

9. Don Hossler and Karen S. Gallagher, "Studying Student College Choice: A Three-Phase Model and the Implications for Policymakers," *College and University* 62 (1987): 207–221.

10. Benjamin L. Castleman, Karen C. Arnold, and Katherine L. Wartman, "Stemming the Tide of Summer Melt: An Experimental Study of the Effects of Post–High School Summer Intervention on Low-Income Students' College Enrollment," *Journal of Research on Educational Effectiveness* 5 (2012): 1–18; Benjamin L. Castleman, Lindsay C. Page, and Korynn Schooley, "The Forgotten Summer: Does the Offer of College Counseling After High School Mitigate Summer Melt Among College-Intending, Low-Income high School Graduates?" *Journal of Policy Analysis and Management* 33 (2014): 320–344.

11. B. J. Casey, Rebecca M. Jones, and Leah H. Somerville, "Braking and Accelerating of the Adolescent Brain," *Journal of Research on Adolescence* 21, no. 1 (2011): 21–33.

12. Castleman, Arnold, and Wartman, "Stemming the Tide of Summer Melt"; Castleman, Page, and Schooley, "The Forgotten Summer"; Benjamin L. Castleman and Lindsay C. Page, "Summer Nudging: Can Personalized Text Messages and Peer Mentor Outreach Increase College Going Among Low-Income High School Graduates?" (working paper, Center for Education Policy and Workforce Competitiveness, University of Virginia, Charlottesville VA, 2013).

CHAPTER 1

1. Karen C. Arnold, Shezwae Fleming, Mario DeAnda, Benjamin L. Castleman, and Katherine L. Wartman, "The Summer Flood: The Invisible Gap Among Low-Income Students," *Thought and Action*, Fall 2009, 23–34.

2. Ibid.

3. At the time of Arnold's interviews, students verified the information on their FAFSA directly with USDOE. The verification process has subsequently changed, and students are now required to verify the information on their FAFSA directly with each institution to which they have been accepted.

4. Benjamin L. Castleman, Karen C. Arnold, and Katherine L. Wartman, "Stemming the Tide of Summer Melt: An Experimental Study of the Effects of Post–High School Summer Intervention on Low-Income Students' College Enrollment," *Journal of Research on Educational Effectiveness* 5 (2012): 1–18.

5. Christopher Avery and Thomas J. Kane, "Student Perceptions of College Opportunities. The Boston COACH Program," in *College Choices: The Economics of Where to Go, When to Go, and How to Pay for It*, ed. Caroline M. Hoxby (Chicago, IL: University of Chicago Press, 2004), 355–394.

6. American School Counselor Association, "Student-to-School-Counselor Ratios" (unpublished report, 2012), http://www.schoolcounselor.org/content.asp?contentid=658.

7. Melissa E. Clinedinst and David A. Hawkins, "State of College Admission" (unpublished report, National Association for College Admission Counseling, Washington, DC, 2009).

8. Benjamin L. Castleman, Lindsay C. Page, and Korynn Schooley, "The Forgotten Summer: Does the Offer of College Counseling After High School Mitigate Summer Melt Among College-Intending, Low-Income high School Graduates?" *Journal of Policy Analysis and Management* 33 (2014): 320–344.

9. Richard Thaler and Cass Sunstein, *Nudge: Improving Decisions About Health, Wealth, and Happiness* (New Haven, CT: Yale University Press, 2008).

10. Arnold et al., "The Summer Flood."

11. Benjamin L. Castleman and Lindsay C. Page, "A Trickle or A Torrent? Understanding the Extent of Summer 'Melt' Among College-Intending High School Graduates," *Social Science Quarterly* 95, no. 1 (March 2014), http://onlinelibrary .wiley.com/doi/10.1111/ssqu.12032/pdf.

12. Ibid.; Chris Matthews, Korynn Schooley, and Niveen Vosler, "Proposal for a Summer Transition Program to Increase FCS College-Going Rates" (unpublished report, Fulton County Schools, Fulton County, GA); Lindsay Daugherty, "An Evaluation of Summer Link, a Counseling Program to Facilitate College-Going" (paper presented at the fall conference of the Association of Policy Analysis and Management, Baltimore, MD, November 2011).

13. Castleman, Page, and Schooley, "The Forgotten Summer."

14. Martha J. Bailey and Susan M. Dynarski, "Inequality in Postsecondary Education," in *Whither Opportunity? Rising Inequality and the Uncertain Life Chances of Low-Income Children*, eds. Greg J. Duncan and Richard J. Murnane (New York: Russell Sage Foundation, 2012), 117–132; Jonathan Smith, Matea Pender, and Michael Hurwitz, "The Full Extent of Academic Under-Match," *Economics of Education Review* 32 (2013): 247–261.

CHAPTER 2

1. The profiles of Adam, Tarik, and Alicia, and of students in subsequent chapters, describe real people. To protect their identities we have used pseudonyms and have been intentionally general in our geographic descriptions of where they live. The two exceptions to this rule occur in chapter 6, where the Bridge to College coaches we profile gave us explicit permission to use their real identities.

CHAPTER 3

1. American Student Assistance, "Understanding the FAFSA Verification Process," April 22, 2011, http://www.asa.org/articles/2011/april/understanding-the -fafsa-verification-process.aspx.

2. Sendhil Mullainathan and Eldar Shafir, *Scarcity: Why Having Too Little Means So Much* (New York: Times Books, 2013).

CHAPTER 4

1. For further details, see Benjamin L. Castleman, Lindsay C. Page, and Korynn Schooley, "The Forgotten Summer: Does the Offer of College Counseling After High School Mitigate Summer Melt Among College-Intending, Low-Income

high School Graduates?" *Journal of Policy Analysis and Management* 33 (2014): 320–344.

2. There were students who had an assessed expected family contribution of zero, based on the information provided on their FAFSA (Free Application for Federal Financial Aid).

3. These were students with expected family contributions large enough to make them ineligible for a Pell grant.

4. For a detailed account of the development of Summer PACE in Fulton, see Lynn Jenkins, Michelle Wisdom, and Sarah Glover, "Increasing College-Going Rates in Fulton County Schools: A Summer Intervention Based on the Strategic Use of Data," Cases in Education: Data Use (Cambridge, MA: Harvard Education Press, 2012).

5. Lindsay Daugherty, "An Evaluation of Summer Link, A Counseling Program to Facilitate College-Going (working paper, presented at the 2012 Fall Conference of the Association of Policy Analysis and Management, Baltimore, MD, 2012).

CHAPTER 5

1. Robert M. Bond, Christopher J. Fariss, Jason J. Jones, Adam D. I. Kramer, Cameron Marlow, Jaime E. Settle, and James H. Fowler, "A 61-Million-Person Experiment in Social Influence and Political Mobilization," *Nature* 489 (2012): 295–298.

2. Amanda Lenhardt, "Teens, Smart Phones, and Texting" (unpublished report, Pew Research Center, Washington, DC, 2012).

3. Richard Thaler and Cass Sunstein, *Nudge: Improving Decisions About Health, Wealth, and Happiness* (New Haven, CT: Yale University Press, 2008); Dean Karlan, Margaret McConnell, Sendhil Mullainathan, and Jonathan Zinman, "Getting to the Top of Mind: How Reminders Increase Saving" (National Bureau of Economic Research Working Paper No. 16205, Cambridge, MA, 2010); M. S. Stockwell, E. O. Kharbanda, R. A. Martinez, C. Y. Vargas, D. K. Vawdrey, and S. Camargo, "Effects of a Text Messaging Intervention on Influenza Vaccination in an Urban, Low-Income Pediatric and Adolescent Population," *Journal of the American Medical Association* 307, no. 16 (2012): 1702–1708.

4. Brigitte C. Madrian and Dennis F. Shea, "The Power of Suggestion: Inertia in 401(k) Participation and Savings Behavior," *Quarterly Journal of Economics* 116, no. 4 (2001): 1149–1187.

5. Peter Bergman, "Parent-Child Information Frictions and Human Capital Investment: Evidence from a Field Experiment" (working paper, Teachers College, Columbia University, New York, NY, 2013).

6. Passarella and Lin's original company focused on health care messaging was named Reify Health. Signal Vine is the name of their text messaging enterprise focused on the education sector.

7. Benjamin L. Castleman and Lindsay C. Page, "Summer Nudging: Can Personalized Text Messages and Peer Mentor Outreach Increase College Going

Among Low-Income High School Graduates?" (Center for Education Policy and Workforce Competitiveness Working Paper No. 9, University of Virginia, Charlottesville VA, 2013).

8. Karen C. Arnold, Benjamin L. Castleman, Alexandra Chewning, and Lindsay C. Page, "Advisor and Student Experiences of Summer Support for College-Intending, Low-Income High School Graduates" (paper presented at the fall conference of the Association for the Study of Higher Education, St. Louis, MO, November 2013).

CHAPTER 6

1. The Higher Education Opportunity Program was established in 1969 by the New York State Legislature to support educationally and economically disadvantaged students. The program served 4,600 students in 2011–2012. For details on Skidmore's program, see http://www.skidmore.edu/opportunity_program/missionstmt.php. For details on HEOP in New York State, see http://www.highered.nysed.gov/kiap/colldev/HEOP/.

2. Jacqueline Berman, Lorena Ortiz, and Johannes Bos, "Evaluation of the SOURCE Program: An Intervention to Promote College Application and Enrollment Among Urban Youth" (Oakland, CA: Berkeley Policy Associates, 2008); Scott Carrell and Bruce Sacerdote, "Late Interventions Matter Too: The Case of College Coaching in New Hampshire" (National Bureau of Economic Research Working Paper No. 19031, Cambridge, MA, 2013); Patricia Gándara and Maria Mejorado, "Putting Your Money Where Your Mouth Is: Mentoring as a Strategy to Increase Access to Higher Education," in *Preparing for College: Nine Elements of Effective Outreach*, eds. William G. Tierney, Zoe B. Corwin, and Julia E. Colyar (Albany, NY: State University of New York Press, 2005), 89–110.

3. Students in the uAspire sites received either the personalized text messages or peer mentor outreach, but not both. For further details, see Benjamin L. Castleman and Lindsay C. Page, "Summer Nudging: Can Personalized Text Messages and Peer Mentor Outreach Increase College Going Among Low-Income High School Graduates?" (Center for Education Policy and Workforce Competitiveness Working Paper No. 9, University of Virginia, Charlottesville, VA, 2013).

CHAPTER 7

1. In addition to this book, we have written a handbook on summer melt, sponsored by the Strategic Data Project housed at the Center for Education Policy Research at Harvard University. The aim of the handbook is to provide comprehensive guidance on how educational agencies can assess the extent of summer melt among their students and proactively respond to reduce melt rates. We intend for the handbook to be a more detailed treatment of the topics covered in this chapter. The complete summer melt handbook can be found at http://www.gse.harvard.edu/cepr-resources/files/news-events/sdp-summer-melt-handbook.pdf.

2. Susan M. Dynarski, Steven W. Hemelt, and Joshua M. Hyman, "The Missing Manual: Using National Student Clearinghouse Data to Track Postsecondary

Outcomes" (National Bureau of Economic Research Working Paper No. 19552, 2013).

CHAPTER 8

1. Eric Bettinger, Bridget Terry Long, Philip Oreopoulos, and Lisa Sanbonmatsu, "The Role of Application Assistance and Information in College Decisions: Results from the H&R Block FAFSA Experiment," *Quarterly Journal of Economics* 127, no. 3 (2012): 1205–1242.

2. Federal Student Aid, USDOE, "FAFSA Completion by High School," http://studentaid.ed.gov/about/data-center/student/application-volume/fafsa -completion-high-school.

3. ACT, "ACT and Statewide Testing," http://www.act.org/stateservices/; College Board, "The SAT School Day," http://professionals.collegeboard.com/higher-ed/recruitment/sat-test/school-day.

4. Internal College Board report shared via personal correspondence with Jessica Howell, executive director for policy research at the College Board, February 7, 2014.

5. Michael Hurwitz, Jonathan Smith, Sunny Niu, and Jessica Howell, "The Maine Question: How Is Four-Year College Enrollment Affected by Mandatory College Entrance Exams?" *Educational Evaluation and Policy Analysis*, March 5, 2014; Daniel Klasik, "The ACT of Enrollment: The College Enrollment Effects of Required College Entrance Exam Taking," *Educational Researcher* 42, no. 3 (2013): 151–160; George Bulman, "The Effect of Access to College Assessments on Enrollment and Attainment" (working paper, Stanford University, 2013).

6. William G. Bowen, Matthew M. Chingos, and Michael S. McPherson, *Crossing the Finish Line: Completing College at America's Public Universities* (Princeton, NJ: Princeton University Press, 2009); Alexandria Radford, *Top Student, Top School? How Social Class Shapes Where Valedictorians Go to College* (Chicago, IL: University of Chicago Press, 2013).

7. Caroline Hoxby and Sarah Turner, "Expanding College Opportunities for High-Achieving, Low Income Students" (working paper, Stanford Institute for Economic Policy Research, Discussion Paper No. 12-014, 2013).

8. College Board, 2013 Fall Counselor Workshops, "4 or More," http://counselorworkshops.collegeboard.org/apply-to-four-or-more.

9. College Goal Sunday, http://www.collegegoalsundayusa.org/Pages/default .aspx.

10. HCM Strategists, "The American Dream 2.0: How Financial Aid Can Help Improve College Access, Affordability, and Completion," http://www.hcmstrategists .com/americandream2-0/report/HCM_Gates_Report_1_17_web.pdf.

CONCLUSION

1. SHEEO, *State Higher Education Finance, Fiscal Year 2012: A Project of the Staff of the State Higher Education Executive Officers* (Boulder, CO: SHEEO, 2013).

2. Sandy Baum, Jennifer Ma, and Kathleen Payea, *Education Pays 2013: The Benefits of Education to Individuals and Society* (New York: The College Board, 2013).

3. Martha J. Bailey and Susan M. Dynarski, "Inequality in Postsecondary Education," in *Whither Opportunity? Rising Inequality and the Uncertain Life Chances of Low-Income Children*, eds. Greg J. Duncan and Richard J. Murnane (New York: Russell Sage Foundation, 2012), 117–132; Jonathan Smith, Matea Pender, and Michael Hurwitz, "The Full Extent of Academic Under-Match," *Economics of Education Review* 32 (2013): 247–261.

ACKNOWLEDGMENTS

We had the luck of beginning our collaboration on summer melt while we were both graduate students at the Harvard Graduate School of Education. In addition, we were next-door neighbors, both serving as Harvard College freshman proctors (academic and residential advisors for the first-year students), and both of us parents of little girls who were only weeks apart in age. Needless to say, we have spent a great deal of time together over the past several years in a variety of contexts and have enjoyed our growing friendship and ongoing professional collaboration through the many intersections of our lives.

Karen Arnold, professor at the Boston College Lynch School of Education, deserves credit for applying the term "summer melt" to the phenomenon of college-intending high school graduates failing to enroll in college. Karen's pioneering work identified this pattern and motivated our own work in this area. We have had the benefit of building on her foundation ever since. We are also grateful to Dennis Littky and Nancy Diaz Bain, codirectors of the Met Center in Providence, Rhode Island. Their commitment to students continues long after they have walked across the graduation stage, and the Met's work on summer melt emerged largely as a result of their determination to help all students succeed in their postsecondary aspirations.

Our work on summer melt has been indelibly shaped by our ongoing collaboration with the nonprofit organization uAspire and its phenomenal organizational leadership. We have now worked with uAspire for almost five years across several different interventions. One of the attributes that we most respect and appreciate is their dedication to providing high-quality support to the students they serve. They have a coherent vision for how to guide students to and through college and are dedicated to implementing this vision with fidelity.

At uAspire, we particularly thank Bob Giannino-Racine and Erin Cox for their willingness to take a risk and work with us on the initial summer counseling intervention, even though we were still graduate students at the time. We thank them for opening up their organization and data to deep inquiry and investigation. We thank Alexandra Chewning for being our veritable partner-in-crime in implementing several summer melt interventions at uAspire and for the generosity with which she has provided feedback on draft chapters of this book. We honor the uAspire advisors and peer mentors for their deep commitment to helping students realize successful and affordable college outcomes.

We thank our several doctoral mentors for both guiding and supporting us in this work: John Willett and Dick Murnane for the excellent training on how to conduct rigorous, real-world research; Tom Kane and Larry Katz for critical feedback; and Chris Avery for his ongoing mentorship and friendship. We thank, in particular, Bridget Terry Long for the many ways in which she has made this body of work possible. Bridget is deeply committed to research and to advancing and supporting her students, and made both our counseling and text messaging interventions possible by generously allocating a portion of her existing grant funds to these projects. We hope to pay forward the generosity of all of these advisors by providing similar depth and quality of support to our own students in the years to come.

This work has also benefited tremendously by our involvement with the Center for Education Policy Research at Harvard University and the Strategic Data Project (SDP) housed therein. Jon Fullerton and Sarah Glover provided unwavering support for the development of our summer melt research. We thank Sarah for the brainchild of the SDP "Summer Melt Handbook" and Ashley

Snowdon for her partnership in its development and production. We thank Patty Diaz-Andrade for leading the SDP Data Fellowship and for facilitating our connection to former SDP fellows Korynn Schooley and Lindsay Daugherty, who developed and led summer melt initiatives in the Fulton County Schools and Fort Worth Independent School District, respectively. We thank Chris Matthews, Niveen Vosler, G. Mark Ellis, and Wayne Bellcross, all of whom were instrumental in the program development and implementation or in the data sharing that facilitated our opportunity to study and write about summer melt in Fulton County. In Fulton, we are grateful to Korynn Schooley for her leadership, partnership, and most especially her friendship.

The implementation of the text messaging campaign benefited from many helping hands. Laura Owen facilitated our collaboration with both the Denver Public Schools and the Dallas Independent School District to implement the text intervention. Eric Bettinger, Bridget Terry Long, and Chris Avery provided feedback on the development of the project ideas. Owen also facilitated our connection to Ralph Pascarella and Michael Lin of Signal Vine, who have been creative partners in developing and honing their text message platform to facilitate digital outreach to students and text-based communication between students and supporting adults.

Several of the interventions discussed throughout this book also would not have been possible without the collaboration of innovative leaders in several partner organizations, including Laura Keane (Mastery Charter Schools); Sylvia Lopez, Dorothea Weir, and Shane Hall (Dallas Independent School District); Cori Canty and Chung Pham (Denver Public Schools); Leslie Kelly, Freida Trujillo, Phyllis Clay, Sade Bonilla, and Tom Genne (Albuquerque Public Schools); Gilbert Zavala and Drew Scheberle (Austin Chamber of Commerce); Greg Cumpton, Chris King, and Heath Prince (Ray Marshall Center at the University of Texas at Austin); Rich Haines (OneLogos Education Solutions); Karen Looby (Austin Independent School District); and Brian Kathman (Signal Vine). We thank these individuals as well as the counselors, peer mentors, and other staff members who contributed immeasurably to the implementation of summer outreach interventions.

Prior to embarking on this book, our work had not focused on capturing the voices of students and the experiences of counselors and other supporting adults working to smooth students' transition from high school to college. We are grateful to the leadership and staff of several organizations that work directly with students for taking the time to share their experiences and stories with us. These include David Johnston at the Center for Higher Education Retention Excellence; Martin Etsey, Carisa Lovejoy, Carla Hawkins, and Zakiya Edens of Career Beginnings, a program of the Hartford Consortium for Higher Education; Alex Bernadotte and the staff of coaches at Beyond12, including Eboni Dunbar, Catherine Cruz Bioc, Cinthya Vieyra, Isabel Glaese, Jazmin Betancourt, Katherine Zepeda, Lara Sidhu, and Nam Nguyen; Laurie Bainter and Lisa Orden Zarin at College Bound St. Louis; Elizabeth Morgan at the National College Access Network; Janice Bloom at CARA NYC; Jesus Prado at Alliance College-Ready Public Schools; Danny Voloch at iMentor; Jessica Kennedy and Adam Green at the West Virginia Higher Education Policy Commission; Jen Fox at the Minnesota Office of Higher Education; and Ritu Sen, Cassie Magesis, Emily Rotando, Tracey Ann Guillaume, Kimberly Bray, Elizabeth Kelly, Alan Miyakawa, and the peer coaches, including Yabielis Guerrero and Yoscar Ogando, at the Urban Assembly and Bridge to College. Our understanding of the causes and consequences of summer melt has been strengthened enormously by the contributions and insights of these individuals and their organizations.

Several aspects of the research included in this book would not have been possible without the outstanding research and administrative support from a number of individuals, including Cindy Floyd, Zack Mabel, Adam Ganik, Anna Hagen, Jonathon Davis, Luis Miranda, Daniel Grafstein, Kira Nipson, and Bryan Stephany. In addition, we are grateful for the generous financial support of the research discussed throughout the book from the Bill and Melinda

Gates Foundation, the William T. Grant Foundation, the Spencer Foundation, the Christian R. and Mary F. Lindback Foundation, the Heckscher Foundation for Children, the National Association of Student Financial Aid Administrators, the Texas Higher Education Coordinating Board, the Michael and Susan Dell Foundation, and the Kresge Foundation.

We cannot express enough gratitude to Caroline Chauncey at Harvard Education Press for her editorial guidance and encouragement throughout our writing process. Whenever we were stuck, Caroline was always at the ready with just the right piece of advice to keep us going.

Finally, we give thanks for the love and support of our spouses, Celia Castleman and Brad Molyneaux, and for the joy that our children, Lila and Simon Castleman and Nora and Caleb Molyneaux, bring to our lives each day.

ABOUT THE AUTHORS

BENJAMIN L. CASTLEMAN is an assistant professor of education and public policy at the University of Virginia. His work applies insights from behavioral economics to help students and their families navigate complex educational decisions, and focuses primarily on improving college access and success for low-income and first-generation college students.

LINDSAY C. PAGE is an assistant professor of education and a research scientist at the Learning Research and Development Center at the University of Pittsburgh. Her work focuses on quantitative methods and their application to questions regarding the effectiveness of educational policies and programs across the preschool to postsecondary spectrum.

INDEX